Discovering
English County Regiments

Ian F. W. Beckett

By altars old their banners fade
Beneath dear spires; their names are set
In minster aisle, in yew tree shade;
Their memories fight for England yet.

Front cover: The 5th Foot at the Peninsular War battle of Busaco, 1810.

Back cover: 'The Herefordshire Regiment in Gallipoli' (see page 49).

ACKNOWLEDGEMENTS
In preparing this edition, the author has been greatly assisted by the curators of regimental museums. Special thanks are due to: Martin Boswell, Richard Callaghan, Major J. R. Chapman MBE, David Chilton, Yolanda Corts, Martin Crowther, Geoffrey Crump, Major C. M. J. Deedes, Major Richard Dinnin, Peter Donnelly, Peter Duckers MA, Lieutenant Colonel David Eliot, Major John Ellis, Rupert Gaze, Lieutenant Colonel M. J. Glover MA AMA, Helen Gurney, Major J. O. M. Hackett, Major James N. Hereford, Colonel T. J. B. Hill, David Hopkins, Mrs Penelope James, Mrs Helen Jones, Lieutenant Colonel Hugh Keatinge OBE, J. P. Kelleher MA, Guy Kilminster, John Lowles, Nigel Lutt, Captain P. H. D. Marr, Lieutenant Colonel Neil McIntosh MBE, Major Richard Miles, Major R. G. Mills, Karl Noble, Geoff Preece, Major R. S. Prophet, Lieutenant Colonel John Sainsbury OBE, Lieutenant Colonel A. J. Scott MBE, Stephen D. Shannon, George C. Streatfield, Colonel Anthony Swallow OBE, Kate Thaxton, Colonel John Tillett, Lieutenant Colonel T. C. E. Vines, Major Richard Vyvyan-Robinson MBE, Colonel H. B. H. Waring OBE, Colonel Peter Worthy.
Illustrations are acknowledged as follows: Ian F. W. Beckett, pages 98 and 108; Bedfordshire and Luton Archives and Records Service, page 14; The Guardians of The Cambridgeshire Regiment Collection, pages 21 and 22; The Durham Light Infantry Museum and Durham Art Gallery, pages 36 and 38; Fort Ticonderoga Museum, pages 6 and 130; The Fusiliers Museum of Northumberland, pages 7, 91 and front cover; The Green Howards Regimental Museum, pages 136 and 137; The Herefordshire Light Infantry Museum, page 48 and back cover; Hertford Museum, page 50; Illustrated London News, page 32; The Keep Military Museum, Dorchester, page 33; King's Own Royal Regiment Museum, Lancaster, pages 60 and 62; The King's Own Yorkshire Light Infantry Museum, Doncaster Museum and Art Gallery, pages 139 and 141; Cadbury Lamb, pages 20, 34, 73 (both), 81, 87 and 119; Media Ops, Land Command (photograph by Captain Jim Gallagher, RLC), page 138; Museum of the Queen's Lancashire Regiment, pages 57, 58, 68, 70 and 71; The Prince of Wales's Own Regiment of Yorkshire, pages 133, 134, 142 and 143; The Queen's Royal Surrey Regiment Museum, pages 112 and 115; Redcoats in the Wardrobe, The Royal Gloucestershire, Berkshire and Wiltshire Regiment (Salisbury) Museum, pages 17, 18, 124 and 126; The Regimental Museum, The Duke of Cornwall's Light Infantry, pages 26 and 27; The Royal Hampshire Regiment Museum, pages 45 and 46; The Royal Regiment of Fusiliers, pages 120 and 121; The Shropshire Regimental Museum Trust, pages 8, 82, 101 (both); Soldiers of Gloucestershire Museum, pages 41 and 42; The Staffordshire Regiment Museum, pages 105 and 107; The Worcestershire and Sherwood Foresters Regiment, pages 94, 95, 127 and 128; The York and Lancaster Regiment, page 144.
The author is indebted to the original work of Arthur Taylor in the first two editions of this book.

Use the Internet for FREE at
all Essex Libraries

Essex County Council
Libraries

CONTENTS

INTRODUCTION

Writing about the Peninsular War (1808–14), the late Sir Arthur Bryant once referred to the British army's 'great, undemonstrative regiments of the line'. Guardsmen, Riflemen, Highlanders and sundry specialists have often grabbed the most public attention, but it was the ordinary, unpretentious line regiments who were the real backbone of the army. Moreover, as suggested in the first edition of *Discovering English County Regiments*, the county and England are synonymous. Characterised by Arthur Taylor (author of the first edition) as 'the object and source of honest local loyalty', the county as an administrative unit dates back to the Anglo-Saxon kingdoms. By comparison, county regiments are a very recent creation but, over time, they have become an essential ingredient of English county identity and, thus, of English national identity. As Arthur Taylor again suggested, it was a happy and fortuitous decision to forge formal links between counties and regiments. Indeed, the county regiment has become part of the very fabric of England.

In 1660, when King Charles II returned from exile to reclaim his throne, two very different English armies existed: the remnants of Parliament's New Model Army in England, Dunkirk and Ireland; and Charles's own army of exiles, also in Dunkirk. The New Model Army was largely disbanded, with some elements sent to garrison Tangier, part of the wedding dowry of Charles's Portuguese queen, Catherine of Braganza, and others to Portugal. A few units were incorporated with the exiled Royalist army into new regiments of Foot Guards and Horse. In theory, the restored Royal Army remained very small, only nine regiments of foot being raised on the permanent English establishment. A further forty-one regiments of foot were raised temporarily for the English establishment at various times during the Second and Third Anglo-Dutch Wars (1665–7, 1672–4) and the brief English participation in the Franco-Dutch War (1672–8). Scotland and Ireland retained separate military establishments, while English contingents also served the Portuguese, the Dutch between 1660 and 1665 and between 1674 and 1685, and the French between 1672 and 1678. Included among those regiments raised for Charles II were the later 1st–6th, 18th, and 21st Foot, of which the 1st Foot had a second battalion. Two of them – the 2nd and the 4th Foot – were raised specifically for the defence of Tangier.

There was another significant expansion of the regiments of foot in 1685, when King James II authorised the raising of nine new regiments on the English establishment (including the later 7th–15th Foot) in response to the rebellion of the Duke of Monmouth. This was followed three years later by the raising of eight more (including the later 16th–17th, 19th–20th, 22nd–23rd Foot) as he faced the threat of invasion by William of Orange. There were also smaller increases in the Scottish and Irish establishments. William's accession to the throne after James's expulsion committed England to what became known as the 'Nine Years War', or the War of the League of Augsburg (1689–97). The former Anglo-Dutch Brigade returned to the English establishment and the army was also expanded by the additions of more new regiments (including the later 24th–28th and 35th–36th Foot). At the end of the war Parliament acted to reduce the establishment but, under Queen Anne, during the War of Spanish Succession (1702–14) no fewer than sixty-nine new regiments of horse or foot (including the later 29th–34th and 37th Foot) were raised.

Apart from those troops regarded as being for 'Guards and Garrisons' and the army in Flanders, there was also the so-called 'Augmentation', whereby additional forces were jointly funded by England and the Netherlands, of which only a third were subjects of the Crown. Further subsidies also maintained allied contingents in

A grenadier of the 47th Foot during the Seven Years War. Raised as Mordaunt's Regiment, it ultimately became part of The Loyal Regiment (North Lancashire).

Portugal and Spain. With the end of the war came the customary reduction. At the height of the War of Spanish Succession there were sixty-three English regiments of foot, nineteen Irish and three Scottish. Of these, only thirty-six English, five Irish and one Scottish still survived by 1714.

Before the beginning of the War of Austrian Succession (1740–8), only a few more regiments (including the later 40th–41st Foot) were added to what had formally become the British army in 1707. With the renewal of war, however, more regiments were raised (including the later 43rd–49th Foot). In 1751 numbers were formally allocated to the regiments of foot and it became usual to refer to them by their number rather than, as previously, by the name of their colonel.

On the approach of renewed European hostilities in 1755, further regiments were raised (including the later 50th–60th Foot). Then, in August 1756, following the beginning of what became the Seven Years War (1756–63), fifteen of the existing sixty regiments of foot were authorised to raise a second battalion. In one of the typically complicated arrangements of the time, two regiments raised specifically for service in North America (the original 50th and 51st Foot) were disbanded in 1757 and eleven junior regiments (previously 52nd–62nd) were renumbered (50–60th Foot). Another regiment raised in North America, the Royal American Regiment, was originally numbered the 62nd Regiment before being counted separately as the 60th Rifles (later the King's Royal Rifle Corps).

In 1758 the new second battalions were numbered in their own right (from 61st to 75th Foot), though the last five were subsequently disbanded in 1763. In 1775 there was a further increase of thirty-five regiments of foot authorised for the American War of Independence. Many were disbanded in 1783 though some survived (the later 71st–73rd Foot) and some Highland regiments then came into existence in 1786 and 1787 (the later 74th–77th Foot). Another development of the American War was the first attempt to link regiments with counties – intended, according to the official circular of 31st August 1782, to 'cultivate and improve connections so as to create a mutual attraction between the County and the Regiment which may at all times be useful towards recruiting the Regiment'. In many cases, however, there was little real association between county and regiment. Some colonels declined to act in accordance with the spirit of the circular when some counties were more likely to produce recruits than others, and it was difficult to make the scheme definitive, especially as there were the additional problems of accommodating recruitment for the cavalry and the Guards. In the event, more general recruiting rules had to be authorised in June 1783, effectively killing off what was later to be called 'territorialisation'.

Another massive expansion of the army occurred as a result of the French Revolutionary and Napoleonic Wars (1793–1815). There was a redistribution of regimental numbers in 1793 and many new regiments came into existence (including the later 78th–93rd Foot), as well as many second or even third battalions of existing regiments. The usual contraction followed the end of the wars, with second battalions being disbanded once more. In 1816, the 95th Rifles (later The Rifle Brigade), raised in 1800, was entirely separated from the list of numbered regiments, the number being reallocated when six new regiments appeared in 1823–4 (94th–99th Foot). Under the pressure of the Indian Mutiny (1857–8), second battalions were revived for twenty-three regiments (2nd–24th Foot), with a new regiment (100th Foot) also raised in addition to more battalions for the 60th Rifles and Rifle Brigade. A second battalion was authorised for the 25th Foot in 1859, while nine European regiments (101st–109th) formerly in the service of the

The Relief of Lucknow in 1857 during the Indian Mutiny.

7

East India Company were transferred to the British establishment in 1861–2 following the Company's abolition.

As part of the Cardwell reforms (Edward Cardwell was Secretary for War 1868–74), battalions were linked in 1872 in what was termed 'localisation', in which two regular battalions, two militia battalions and a number of volunteer battalions were grouped into districts served by a single depot. The idea was that one regular battalion would be stationed at home and supply drafts and reliefs to the other regular battalion overseas while the militia and volunteers would benefit from their greater exposure to the regulars through the brigade depot. In fact, the balance of battalions at home and overseas could never be attained through the army's increasing imperial commitments. Nevertheless, despite the evident problems, in July 1881 localisation was converted into full territorialisation, whereby the battalions were to be permanently linked as new county regiments. Militia and volunteer battalions also became officially part of the new territorialised county regiments as additional battalions.

When territorialisation commenced, only the first twenty-five infantry regiments in the Army List had second battalions. From the remaining eighty-three single-battalion regiments, forty-one new double-battalion regiments were formed, leaving only the 79th Foot (The Cameron Highlanders) as a single-battalion regiment (until 1897). All sixty-six double-battalion regiments that now existed, as well as the 79th Foot, were given a territorial distinction, forty-six of them in England, ten in Scotland, eight in Ireland and three in Wales. In some cases the new regiments did retain the previously nominal county affiliation accorded them in 1782; in other cases, however, regiments were entirely divorced from their previous county affiliations. To give but one example, the 14th Foot, affiliated to Buckinghamshire since 1809, now became the 1st Battalion, The West Yorkshire Regiment.

None the less, despite the often bogus nature of the new county affiliations and the fact that they did not by any means recruit exclusively or even primarily in their

Officer cadets at Sandhurst, 1870, wearing the distinctive French-style shako of 1869–78 with the badge plate of the Royal Military College.

counties, the regiments as they were created in 1881 became in all respects the English county regiments of popular memory and affection. In many respects it was the First World War that truly established this affectionate link between county and regiment. On the one hand there was the existing link provided by the militia and the volunteers, which had become the Special Reserve and the Territorial Force respectively under the Haldane reforms in 1908 (Richard Burdon Haldane was Secretary of State for War 1905–12). On the other hand the decision in August 1914 to raise a new wartime army outside the machinery provided by the County Territorial Associations was accomplished by creating service battalions of the county regiments. Though not managed in quite the same way, a similar solution was applied during the Second World War.

Following the reduction of the wartime army, and despite the retention of wartime conscription in the form of national service and seemingly still widening commitments, there was a considerable reduction in the number of regular battalions in 1948–9. Most regiments amalgamated their 1st and 2nd Battalions in what was termed placing the second battalions in 'suspended animation'. It was but the beginning of a continuing process as decolonisation gathered pace. Cavalry regiments had been subjected to amalgamation at the end of the First World War with the emergence of the so-called 'vulgar fractions', such as the 14th/20th King's Hussars and 17th/21st Lancers. The same solution was now applied to the infantry in the wake of the Sandys Defence White Paper of April 1957, which envisaged the withdrawal of further overseas garrisons and the termination of national service from 1960, so that the last national serviceman left the army in 1963.

The first wave of amalgamations occurred in 1958–9 within the large brigades (in England: Home Counties, Lancastrian, Yorkshire and Northumberland, Midland, East Anglian, Wessex, Light Infantry, Green Jackets and Mercian) previously established in 1946. The total number of infantry regiments was reduced by means of thirty regiments amalgamating to form fifteen new regiments, each brigade being reduced to three or four regiments. Those selected for amalgamation were not chosen on the basis of seniority, but on the supposed recruiting potential of the brigade area. Brigade cap badges were now to be worn though regiments would retain their own collar badges, belts and shoulder titles. In the 1960s, alongside savage cuts in the Territorial Army, a further expedient was to create multi-battalion large regiments from some of the brigades, hence the emergence of The Light Infantry (1968) from the Light Infantry Brigade, less The Oxfordshire and Buckinghamshire Light Infantry, which joined the former regiments of the Green Jacket Brigade (The Rifle Brigade and The King's Royal Rifle Corps) in The Royal Green Jackets (1966). Similarly, The Royal Anglian Regiment (1964) emerged from The East Anglian Brigade, while The Home Counties Brigade became The Queen's Regiment (1966), with the exception of The Royal Fusiliers (City of London Regiment), which became part of another large combination, The Royal Regiment of Fusiliers (1968). In turn, two or three of the new large regiments or brigades were to be placed in divisions. The York and Lancaster Regiment chose to disband in 1968 rather than face amalgamation.

There have been other amalgamations since, such as the addition of The Royal Hampshire Regiment to The Queen's Regiment in The Princess of Wales's Royal Regiment (Queen's and Royal Hampshires) in 1992. Moreover, the multi-battalion regiments have themselves been steadily reduced in size. Indeed, only three English county regiments remain as they existed in 1881: The Green Howards (Alexandra, Princess of Wales's Own Yorkshire Regiment), which can trace a direct lineage from 1688; The 22nd (Cheshire) Regiment, which can trace a direct lineage from 1689; and The Duke of Wellington's Regiment (West Riding), created in 1881 from the union of the 33rd Foot (1702) and 76th Foot (1787). Sadly, it is not entirely inconceivable that, in the long term, some of the existing seven Divisions (Guards, Scottish, Queen's, King's, Prince of Wales's, Royal Irish, and Light) may eventually be reduced to single regiments.

The regimental system has been frequently criticised but, in reality, it was a better solution to the requirements of a global empire than continental-style corps and divisions. Moreover, it was one of the principal factors that maintained the morale of the British army in conditions in which that of others collapsed. Through the twentieth century, the regimental system came under increasing threat from the demands of mass modern warfare in two world wars and, after 1945, from the impact of developments in military technology. Combined arms battle-groups are now the norm in medium- and high-intensity conflict, though the individual battalion still remains the best structure in the kind of low-intensity conflict embracing counter-insurgency and peace-keeping tasks that is still so highly prevalent in contemporary conflict. It has also been argued that the persistence of 'tribal' loyalties in terms of campaigns to save individual regiments or battalions has rendered the army less able to defend itself collectively against the continuing process of reduction.

It may be that technological change combined with socio-economic pressures may eventually undermine the continuing viability of the regimental system. That would be a great pity. Traditions, of course, can be invented, and there is more than an element of invention in many individual regimental traditions. They should be celebrated no less for that, for it should not be forgotten that the traditions of the regiment have a very particular purpose. Field Marshal Viscount Slim once recalled the story of one of his soldiers, when he was serving with a battalion of The Royal Warwickshire Regiment in Mesopotamia during the First World War, rallying the remainder at a desperate moment by crying, 'Show the — yer cap badges.' As Slim wrote, 'They had no cap badges for we wore Wolseley helmets, but they heard the only appeal that could have reached them – to their regiment, the last hold of the British soldier when all else had gone.' Another distinguished soldier, Field Marshal Lord Birdwood, whose first regiment was the 12th Royal Lancers before he transferred to the Indian Army, wrote in 1942: 'Let us preserve our British regimental traditions with all our care, and cherish their separate glories, for they are a precious part of our heritage .... Men live for them, and small as they may seem, will die for them.'

KEY TO THE REGIMENTAL ENTRIES

The entries are standardised but may not all be relevant to every regiment. Consequently, not every entry will necessarily have all elements included.

TITLE

The regimental title given is that borne at the moment of the regiment's final existence as a separate entity before amalgamation or disbandment. As indicated in the Introduction, three regiments still survived unscathed in 2003.

ORIGINS AND DEVELOPMENT

A brief outline of the evolution of the regiment is given.

HISTORY

Space precludes more than a summary of some of the more interesting aspects of the regiment's past. A word should be said about some aspects of the nomenclature used with regard to battalions. It should be noted that, before 1881, if a second or third battalion of a regiment of foot was raised, the nomenclature would be rendered, for example, as the 1/13th and 2/13th Foot. During the First World War, three 'lines' of the Territorial Force (TF) were mobilised so that, generally, there were 1st, 2nd and 3rd line units of each Territorial battalion. In the case of the 4th Battalion (TF) of The Oxfordshire and Buckinghamshire Light Infantry, for example, these would be rendered as the 1/4th, 2/4th and 3/4th OBLI. Service battalions would be numbered sequentially after the Territorial battalions as, for example, in the case of the 5th, 6th and 7th (Service) Battalions, OBLI. In the Second World War, battalions were again numbered sequentially after Territorial battalions. The Territorial Army (TA) had been doubled in size in 1938, again leading in some cases to the appearance of battalions such as the new 2/6th, The Queen's Royal Regiment (West Surrey) alongside the 6th Battalion, which now became the 1/6th Battalion.

VICTORIA CROSSES

The number awarded the regiment by war or campaign. In addition, there is an indication of how many of the Victoria Crosses are displayed in the regimental museum.

NICKNAMES

Regimental nicknames are given along with their origins.

BADGE

Before 1881, regimental badges were generally based on the regiment's number, with other devices or honours borne on the Colours. With the establishment of the new county regiments in 1881 new badges were devised, usually reflecting the pasts of both linked regiments as appropriate. The now familiar cap badges were introduced with the new field dress after the South African War.

MOTTO

Regimental mottoes are given as emblazoned on the Colours or, occasionally, the badge.

CUSTOMS

Particular traditions associated with each regiment are outlined.

11

FACINGS
The facings given are those of the regiment after 1881.

REGIMENTAL MARCHES
The traditional marches associated with the regiment are listed.

COLOURS
The whereabouts are given of previous Colours laid up or otherwise preserved.

MEMORIALS
Particular monuments are listed that are noteworthy to the regiment in question.

BATTLE HONOURS
Battle honours are those borne on the Colours. Few were awarded in the eighteenth century but after 1801 they began increasingly to be so. It should be noted, however, that many earlier battle honours were awarded by committees that reported in 1881 and 1909. Thus, the honours for Marlborough's victories of Blenheim, Ramillies, Oudenarde and Malplaquet were awarded in 1881. In the two world wars, many more battle honours were awarded than could be carried on the Colours. The Middlesex Regiment, for example, won eighty-three battle honours between 1914 and 1918. Consequently, as a result of decisions in 1922 and 1956 respectively, each regiment selected a representative ten honours from each war to be borne on the Colours, and it is these that are recorded here. It also became the practice in the twentieth century to carry the battle honours for the two world wars on the King's or Queen's Colour and others on the Regimental Colour.

LATER LINEAGE
The lineage of former county regiments in the modern army is given.

MUSEUMS
Address, telephone and other contact numbers are detailed. While the museums listed are open to the public, visiting hours may be restricted and, indeed, in some cases, appointments must be made. It is advisable, therefore, to check in advance.

The regiments are listed alphabetically by county.

BEDFORDSHIRE

The Bedfordshire and Hertfordshire Regiment
(16th Foot)

ORIGINS AND DEVELOPMENT

The 16th was raised in 1688 as Douglas's Regiment of Foot. Affiliated to Buckinghamshire in 1782, the regiment changed its county affiliation to Bedfordshire in 1809. In 1881, the 16th became The Bedfordshire Regiment. A 2nd Battalion existed from 1858 until 1948. To recognise the contribution of Hertfordshire men to the regiment during the First World War, the title changed to The Bedfordshire and Hertfordshire Regiment in 1919. Amalgamated 1958.

HISTORY

Douglas's Regiment was one of the regiments hastily raised by King James II when faced with the invasion threat from William of Orange. Archibald Douglas himself was an officer of the Royal Scots, from which the nucleus of the new regiment was drawn. A year later, the regiment saw its first action at Walcourt in Flanders, fighting with William's Dutch troops against the French. It distinguished itself in Marlborough's campaigns during the War of Spanish Succession, especially at Blenheim on 13th August 1704, which became the Regimental Day. At the siege of Lille in 1708, Sergeant Littler swam a river under fire to cut the fastenings of a drawbridge with a hatchet, earning himself a commission. During the American War of Independence, the regiment made a gallant but ultimately doomed defence of Pensacola in Florida against the Spanish and French in 1781. Much of its service during the French Revolutionary and Napoleonic Wars was in Surinam on the South American coast. It then spent twenty years in Ceylon and India from 1819. The 1st and 2nd Battalions spent much of the last quarter of the nineteenth century on garrison duty in India. The 1st Battalion served during the Relief of Chitral in 1895, when there was a rebellion by the Pathans on the North West Frontier. One interesting artefact is the mysterious Grogan coconut. Mounted for the regiment in a silver chalice in 1903, it was found beside a skeleton in the Australian bush in the mid nineteenth century. It was inscribed with the regimental crest, scenes of military service and the name of Owen Grogan, who served in the regiment from 1812 to 1829 but who had actually died in Ireland. During the First World War all units of the regiment served on the Western Front, with the exception of the 5th Battalion. In the Second World War, the 1st Battalion helped defend Tobruk against Rommel's Afrika Korps and then became part of Orde Wingate's Chindits, operating behind Japanese lines in Burma. The 2nd Battalion served in Tunisia, helping to repel a heavy German attack at Sidi Nar on 11th April 1943 before also fighting hard at Medjez and Cape Bon. The 5th Battalion was captured at Singapore. While serving in Cyprus in December 1951, men of the 1st Battalion formed a human chain to rescue seamen from the shipwrecked steamship *Porlock Hill*.

VICTORIA CROSSES

First World War (7). Of these, six are displayed in the Regimental Museum.

NICKNAMES

The Old Bucks: from the period between 1782 and 1809 when the 16th Foot was affiliated to Buckinghamshire.

Pioneers of the 1st Battalion, The Bedfordshire Regiment, in India at the time of the Relief of Chitral Expedition. In 1895 the Pathan tribesmen on the North West Frontier revolted and barred the way to the British outpost at Chitral. The 1st Bedfords formed part of the force that successfully relieved the garrison.

The Peace-makers: supposedly from being so often stationed elsewhere during the major wars of the eighteenth and nineteenth centuries. The regiment was in Canada, for example, at the time of Waterloo (1815) and only arrived in France in time to participate in the allied entry into Paris.

BADGE
A Hart crossing a Ford within a Garter on a Maltese Cross, the whole superimposed on an eight-pointed Star. The Hart was based on the ancient badge of the county of Hertfordshire and was borne by the Hertfordshire Militia before being adapted in 1881 by the territorial regiment to which the militia was now linked.

MOTTO
Honi soit qui mal y pense ('Let him who thinks evil of it be ashamed').

CUSTOMS
Having sent a detachment to serve as marines at Cartagena in the Caribbean in 1742, officers wore the 'marine cuff' on their mess dress and 'Rule Britannia' was always played before the British national anthem. During the retreat from Mons in August 1914, the drums of the 1st Battalion were hidden in the village of Paturages to prevent their capture by the Germans. One subsequently recovered in 1919 and known as the 'Mons Drum' was always carried on the right rear flank of the escort to the Colours when on parade. The regimental colours were always black and amber. Amber and red had been associated with the Stuarts but, according to tradition, the regiment had changed the red to black on the death of King James II.

FACINGS
   White.

REGIMENTAL MARCHES
   'Mandolinata'.

COLOURS
   St Paul's Church, Bedford; Church of the Transfiguration, Kempston; St Albans Cathedral; St Mary's Church, Luton; Garrison Church, Warley, Brentwood, Essex.

MEMORIALS
   The Embankment, Bedford (South African War); Church of the Transfiguration, Kempston (First and Second World Wars); St Peter-upon-Cornhill, London; Thaba Nchu, South Africa (2nd Battalion).

BATTLE HONOURS
   Namur 1695, Blenheim, Ramillies, Oudenarde, Malplaquet, Surinam, Chitral, South Africa 1900–02.
   Mons, Marne 1914, Ypres 1914 '15 '17, Loos, Somme 1916 '18, Cambrai 1917 '18, Sambre, France and Flanders 1914–18, Suvla, Gaza.
   Dunkirk 1940, North West Europe 1940, Tobruk Sortie, Belhamed, Tunis, North Africa 1941 '43, Cassino II, Trasimene Line, Italy 1944–5, Chindits.

LATER LINEAGE
   Amalgamated with The Essex Regiment in 1958 as The 3rd East Anglian Regiment. Became 3rd Battalion, The Royal Anglian Regiment in 1964, a four-battalion regiment reduced to three battalions in 1970 and to two battalions in 1992. The 5th Battalion (TA) was amalgamated with the 1st Battalion, The Hertfordshire Regiment, in 1961.

MUSEUMS AND ARCHIVES
   Bedfordshire and Hertfordshire Regiment Museum, Luton Museum and Art Gallery, Wardown Park, Old Bedford Road, Luton LU2 7HA (telephone: 01582 746722; website: www.luton.gov.uk). The regimental papers and photographs are held by *Bedfordshire and Luton Archives and Records Service*, Riverside Building, County Hall, Cauldwell Street, Bedford MK42 9AP (telephone: 01234 228833; website: www.bedfordshire.gov.uk/archive).

BERKSHIRE

The Royal Berkshire Regiment (Princes Charlotte of Wales's) (49th and 66th Foot)

ORIGINS AND DEVELOPMENT

The 49th Foot was raised in 1743 as Trelawney's Regiment for garrison service in the West Indies, while the 66th Foot was raised in 1756 as the 2/19th Foot, being designated the 66th in its own right two years later. In 1782 the 49th was affiliated to Hertfordshire and the 66th to Berkshire, while the 49th also took the title of Princess Charlotte of Wales's in 1817. In 1881 the battalions were brought together as the 1st and 2nd Battalions, The Berkshire Regiment. The Royal title was awarded in 1885 to reward the gallantry of the 1st Battalion at Tofrek in the Sudan. Reduced to a single battalion in 1949. Amalgamated 1959.

HISTORY

The 49th Foot was raised from various garrison companies, known collectively as the Jamaica Volunteers. It distinguished itself when sent back to North America and the Caribbean during the American War of Independence. The 66th Foot saw its first action on Santo Domingo (Haiti) in 1795, where it was much afflicted by disease. During the Anglo-American War (1812–14) the 49th went to Canada, where its former commanding officer, Major-General Sir Isaac Brock, the commander-in-chief in upper Canada, was killed leading his old regiment at Queenstown Heights on 13th October 1812. The 1/66th formed part of the garrison on St Helena during Napoleon's captivity: six grenadiers of the regiment carried his coffin when he died in May 1821. The 1st Berkshires served with great gallantry at Tofrek in the Sudan on 22nd March 1885, winning a unique battle honour in this desperate battle to hold a hastily constructed thorn enclosure or 'zariba' against the Dervishes. Less fortunate, the 66th was practically annihilated in a desperate rearguard action at Maiwand during the Second Afghan War on 27th July 1880. Two officers and nine men made a last stand near the village of Khig, the incident being recorded in a famous painting, *The Last Eleven* by Frank Feller. One reminder is Bobbie, the pet dog of Sergeant Kelly. Wounded and covered in blood, Bobbie made her way to Kandahar. She was brought back to England with the remnants of the regiment and was present at a ceremony at Osborne House when Queen Victoria presented campaign and gallantry medals to some of the survivors of Maiwand. Sadly, she was run over and killed by a cab in Gosport in 1882 but was stuffed and remains on display. In the Second World War, the 1st Battalion took part in the defence of Kohima against the Japanese. Part of 6th Brigade, the battalion fought its way into Kohima to relieve the 4th Battalion, The Queen's Own Royal West Kent Regiment, on 21st April 1944. For five weeks it defended Garrison Hill and engaged in ferocious hand-to-hand fighting around the district commissioner's bungalow and tennis court in conditions reminiscent of the trenches of the First World War.

VICTORIA CROSSES

Crimean War (3); South African War (1); First World War (2). Of these, five are on display in the Regimental Museum.

NICKNAMES

The Farmer's Boys: from recruiting in a rural county.

Queen Victoria with 'Bobbie' and members of the 66th (Berkshire) Regiment who survived the Battle of Maiwand in 1880.

The Biscuit Boys: from the Huntley & Palmer biscuit factory in the depot town of Reading.

BADGE
The China Dragon reflects the service of the 49th in China between 1839 and 1842, while the officers' badge included a coil of rope to commemorate the 49th's service as marines at the naval battle of Copenhagen on 2nd April 1801. The badge was backed by the red 'Brandywine flash', adopted as a result of the participation of the light company of the 49th in a successful night bayonet attack on the American rebels at Paoli on the Brandywine creek on 21st September 1777. The Americans vowed revenge, whereupon the light companies involved dyed their distinguishing green hat feathers red so that they should be easily recognised.

CUSTOMS
The 49th played 'Rule Britannia' after its own regimental march to commemorate its presence at the naval battle of Copenhagen. It was awarded a Naval Crown for its Colours for the same action somewhat belatedly in 1951!

MOTTO
Honi soit qui mal y pense ('Let him who thinks evil of it be ashamed').

FACINGS
Royal blue (from 1885).

REGIMENTAL MARCHES
'The Dashing White Sergeant'.

COLOURS
St Mary's, St George's and St Laurence's Churches, Reading; St Michael's

Church, Wallingford; St Helen's Church, Abingdon; Windsor Castle; Osborne House, Isle of Wight.

MEMORIALS

Forbury Gardens, Reading (Maiwand).

BATTLE HONOURS

St Lucia 1778, Egmont-op-Zee, Copenhagen, Duoro, Talavera, Albuhera, Queenstown, Vittoria, Pyrenees, Nivelle, Nive, Orthes, Peninsula, Alma, Inkerman, Sevastopol, Kandahar 1880, Afghanistan 1879–82, Egypt 1882, Tofrek, Suakin 1885, South Africa 1899–1902.

Mons, Marne 1914, Ypres 1914 '17, Neuve Chapelle, Loos, Arras 1917 '18, Cambrai 1917, Selle, Vittorio Veneto, Doiran 1917 '18.

Dunkirk, Normandy Landing, Rhine, Sicily 1943, Damiano, Anzio, Kohima, Mandalay, Fort Dufferin, Burma 1942 '45.

LATER LINEAGE

Amalgamated in 1959 with The Wiltshire Regiment (Duke of Edinburgh's) as The Duke of Edinburgh's Royal Regiment (Berkshire and Wiltshire). In 1994 there was a further amalgamation with The Gloucestershire Regiment as The Royal Gloucestershire, Berkshire and Wiltshire Regiment.

MUSEUMS

The Royal Gloucestershire, Berkshire and Wiltshire Regiment (Salisbury) Museum, The Wardrobe, 58 The Close, Salisbury, Wiltshire SP1 2EX (telephone: 01722 414536; fax: 01722 421626; website: www.thewardrobe.org.uk).

1st Battalion Royal Berkshire Regiment on patrol in Cyprus during the 1950s.

BUCKINGHAMSHIRE

The Buckinghamshire Battalion, The Oxfordshire and Buckinghamshire Light Infantry (TA)

ORIGINS AND DEVELOPMENT

Buckinghamshire raised eight rifle volunteer corps in 1859–60 in response to a French invasion scare. The separate corps were brought together as the 1st Administrative Battalion in July 1862 and consolidated as the 1st Bucks Volunteers in 1875. In 1881 the battalion resolutely refused to consider itself as the 3rd Volunteer Battalion, Oxfordshire Light Infantry, retaining its Buckinghamshire title. In 1908, at which time The Oxfordshire Light Infantry was redesignated as The Oxfordshire and Buckinghamshire Light Infantry, the 1st Bucks passed into the Territorial Force as The Buckinghamshire Battalion, Oxfordshire and Buckinghamshire Light Infantry. Converted to light anti-aircraft artillery in 1947.

HISTORY

As with many other volunteer units, the Bucks sent a detachment to join a volunteer service company in the South African War, serving with the 1st Battalion, Oxfordshire Light Infantry. In the First World War the 1/1st Bucks Battalion took part in a major attack around Ovilliers and Pozières on the Somme between 21st and 24th July 1916, its action in seizing the latter village on 23rd July being commemorated in a painting by W. B. Wollen now displayed in the National Army Museum. Subsequently, it served in Italy, being one of twelve British units (and the only Territorial battalion) to receive the Italian National Committee's Commemorative Medal. The 2/1st Bucks suffered heavy losses in its first action at Fromelles near Laventie, part of a diversion for the Somme operations, on 18th–19th July 1916. A reminder of family tragedies in the First World War is the stole of the Reverend Charles Phipps, honorary chaplain to the 2/1st Battalion. His son, also Charles Phipps, was killed serving with the battalion at Fromelles on 19th July 1916, while his son-in-law Ivor Stewart-Liberty, also in the 2/1st Bucks, lost a leg in the same action. Another of Phipps's sons died of pneumonia on active service in 1919. In the Second World War, the 1st Bucks was tasked with the defence of Hazebrouck during the retreat to Dunkirk. Less one company detached for service elsewhere, the battalion fought until overwhelmed on 28th May 1940, winning a precious forty-eight hours in terms of delaying the German advance and being praised by the German IV Corps. Reformed in England with around two hundred survivors, the battalion was subsequently converted into No. 6 Beach Group in March 1943. Tasked with securing and controlling one of the beach areas for the allied invasion of Normandy on D-Day (6th June 1944), the battalion landed on Sword Beach. Subsequently, in February 1945 the battalion was designated as a 'T' or Target Force, designed to seize and hold installations of special interest during the advance into Germany. In this capacity it took the Krupps testing ground at Meppen and the transmitter station of William Joyce ('Lord Haw Háw') at Norden in April 1945.

BADGE

The Maltese Cross containing, within the circle, the White Swan of Buckinghamshire, associated with the county since the fifteenth century.

FACINGS

In common with other rifle regiments, the battalion wore black buttons and

The men of Buckinghamshire killed in the South African War are commemorated on Coombe Hill, near Wendover.

equipment, with no facings.

REGIMENTAL MARCHES
'I'm Ninety-Five'.

COLOURS
As a rifle regiment, no Colours were carried.

MEMORIALS
St Mary's Church, Aylesbury; Coombe Hill, near Wendover (Volunteer Service Company, South African War).

BATTLE HONOURS
The battalion had no separate battle honours but shared those of its parent regiment. The 1st Bucks Volunteers, however, had earned South Africa 1900–02 in its own right.

LATER LINEAGE
Becoming the 645th Light Anti-aircraft Regiment in 1947, the regiment was renamed 431st Light Anti-aircraft Regiment in 1955 before being absorbed into the 299 Field Regiment, RA (TA), which was the lineal descendant of the county's yeomanry regiment, The Royal Bucks Hussars, in 1961. The 299 Field Regiment was disbanded in March 1967 but, in theory, the traditions of The Buckinghamshire Battalion had been handed in 1961 to a company of the 4th (Volunteer) Battalion, The Royal Green Jackets, later the 5th (Volunteer) Battalion. In 1999 the 5th (Volunteer) Battalion, The Royal Green Jackets, was amalgamated with two other TA battalions as The Royal Rifle Volunteers.

MUSEUMS
The Buckinghamshire Military Museum, The Old Gaol Museum, Market Hill, Buckingham MK18 1JX (telephone: 01280 823020; website: www.army.mod.uk/ceremonialandheritage/museums). Additional items are also displayed in *Claydon House*, Middle Claydon, Winslow, Buckinghamshire MK18 2EY (telephone: 01296 730349; website: www.nationaltrust.org.uk).

CAMBRIDGESHIRE

The Cambridgeshire Regiment (TA)

ORIGINS AND DEVELOPMENT

Nine corps of Cambridgeshire Rifle Volunteers were raised in 1860 with a further corps in 1862. The separate corps were organised into two administrative battalions in 1860 and 1862, the second of which disappeared in 1872. The 1st Administrative Battalion was consolidated in 1880 as the 1st Cambridgeshire Rifle Volunteers and in 1887 it became the 3rd (Cambridgeshire) Volunteer Battalion, The Suffolk Regiment. In 1908 this became The Cambridgeshire Regiment in the new Territorial Force.

HISTORY

A volunteer service company served with the 1st Battalion, The Suffolk Regiment in South Africa in 1900–1, mostly in the Orange Free State. Initially, they covered the flank of the British advance on the capital of the Transvaal at Pretoria. On their return, each man was granted the freedom of the Borough of Cambridge and presented with a silver goblet and framed scroll. During the First World War the 1/1st Battalion served in France and Flanders, distinguishing itself in the attack on the Schwaben Redoubt on the Somme on 14th–15th October 1916. Sir Douglas Haig described the action as 'one of the finest feats performed by the British army'. With the doubling of the Territorial Army in 1938, the 1st Battalion was recruited in Cambridgeshire and the 2nd Battalion on the Isle of Ely. Both the 1st and 2nd Battalions were committed to the defence of Malaya in 1941, 18th Division being diverted there when *en route* to the Middle East. The situation was already gloomy. Landing earlier than the 1st Battalion, the 2nd Battalion had to fight its way out of

'The Three Must-get-here's'. Three of the Cambridgeshires photographed just before embarkation to Flanders in 1915 for active service. The cap badge is quite prominent as is Sergeant Pull's Imperial Service Badge. Corporal Noble Dewey, on the left, was the regiment's first casualty, killed in action on 4th March 1915.

Cambridge, 1946, on the occasion when the drums that were believed lost when Singapore fell were returned to the custody of the regiment. The gentleman seen handing one of the 'Singapore drums' over to a Cambridgeshire Regiment officer is the father of Red Cross Welfare Officer Mary Taylor, who rediscovered them and shipped them back to England.

encirclement at Batu-Pahat, breaching the Japanese cordon at Senggareng. Consequently, both battalions were lost when Singapore surrendered on 15th February 1942. After three and a half years' captivity, twenty-four officers and 760 other ranks of the regiment had died in action or as prisoners of war on the 'Death Railway' in Thailand.

NICKNAMES

The Fen Tigers: from the Cambridgeshire fens.

BADGE

The Castle of Cambridge with the Arms of Ely superimposed.

CUSTOMS

The regiment believed that its drums were lost in Malaya in 1941 but, three and a half years later, they were found in an outbuilding of the Goodwood Hotel, where they had been hidden by Sergeants Kitson and Morgan. It was resolved that, in memory of those who did not return, they should never be played again but paraded in silence. The wife of the commanding officer of the battalion was entitled to wear the 'Lyon Brooch', a diamond-studded gold version of the regimental badge first designed by the wife of Colonel A. J. Lyon, who commanded from 1902 to 1911.

FACINGS

Though not a Royal regiment, the regiment had the rare privilege of wearing blue facings and retained these even after association with the Suffolk Regiment.

REGIMENTAL MARCHES
'Speed the Plough'.

COLOURS
Ely Cathedral.

MEMORIALS
Ely Cathedral.

BATTLE HONOURS
South Africa 1900–01.
Ypres 1915 '17, Somme 1916 '18, Ancre Heights, Pilckem, Passchendaele, Kemmel, Amiens, Hindenburg Line, Pursuit to Mons, France and Flanders 1915–18.
Jahore, Batu-Pahat, Singapore Island, Malaya 1942.

LATER LINEAGE
Converted to 629 (The Cambridgeshire Regiment) Light Anti-Aircraft Regiment, RA (TA) in 1947 and to 629 (The Cambridgeshire Regiment) Parachute Light Regiment RA (TA) in 1954. Amalgamated with 4th Battalion, The Suffolk Regiment in 1960 as The Suffolk and Cambridgeshire Regiment (TA) but disbanded in 1967. The regimental traditions were continued by a rifle company of the 6th (Volunteer) Battalion of The Royal Anglian Regiment from 1971 to 1992, the 5th (Volunteer) Battalion from 1992 to 1995 and the 6th (Volunteer) Battalion once more from 1995 to 1999, when D (Cambridgeshire) Company, 6th (Volunteer) Battalion, The Royal Anglian Regiment was finally disbanded. The battalion itself was amalgamated with two other TA battalions as The East of England Regiment.

MUSEUMS
The Cambridgeshire Regiment Collection, *Imperial War Museum Duxford*, Cambridge CB2 4QR (telephone: 01223 835000; fax: 01223 837267; website: www.iwm.org.uk). Additional items are displayed at *The Ely Museum*, The Old Gaol, Market Street, Ely, Cambridgeshire CB7 4LS (telephone: 01353 666655; fax: 01353 659259; website: www.ely.org.uk); *The Wisbech and Fenland Museum*, Museum Square, Wisbech, Cambridgeshire PE13 1ES (telephone: 01945 583817; fax: 01945 589050); and *The Suffolk Regiment Museum*, Moyses Hall Museum, Bury St Edmunds, Suffolk IP33 1DX (telephone: 01284 706183; website: www.stedmundsbury.gov.uk).

CHESHIRE

The 22nd (Cheshire) Regiment (22nd Foot)

ORIGINS AND DEVELOPMENT

The 22nd was raised at Chester and on the Wirral in 1689 as the Duke of Norfolk's Regiment. It was affiliated to Cheshire in 1782 and has remained associated with the county ever since. In 1881 it became The Cheshire Regiment. A second battalion existed from 1858 to 1948. It has clung to the unofficial title of the 22nd (Cheshire) Regiment since 1881.

HISTORY

The regiment's first campaign was that against the Jacobite forces of the exiled King James II in Ireland in 1689–91, where it saw service at the battles of the Boyne and Aughrim. It was captured *en masse* while being transported by sea in 1695 but was exchanged in 1696. In the eighteenth century, long periods of garrison service were spent on Jamaica and Minorca. At the battle on the Heights of Abraham before Quebec on 13th September 1759, Major-General James Wolfe died in the arms of Ensign Henry Brown of the 22nd. Returning to North America in 1775 to serve under its own colonel, Thomas Gage, who was both the governor of Massachusetts and British commander-in-chief, the 22nd was present at Bunker Hill on 17th June. It was engaged on Long Island in August 1776 and was part of the force that seized Newport, Rhode Island, in May 1778 and then defended it against the French. Service in the Napoleonic Wars included spells in the West Indies, South Africa, India and on Mauritius. Sent to India in 1841, the 22nd was the only British regiment in Sir Charles Napier's army during the conquest of Scinde. Napier defeated thirty thousand Baluchis at Meeanee (Miani) on 17th February 1843, this becoming the Regimental Day. The victory over the Baluchis led to the annexation of Scinde to India and to Napier's famous pun in a telegram announcing his success, *Peccavi* (Latin for 'I have sinned'). During the First World War, the 1st Battalion particularly distinguished itself at Audregnies on 24th August 1914 during the retreat from Mons, when it was cut off and eventually overrun. The 'Miniature Colour', an annual trophy awarded to the best shooting company in the 1st Battalion from 1911 onwards, was hidden at Audregnies and retrieved in 1918. The 12th Battalion won the French Croix de Guerre for its part in the attack on 'Pip Ridge' during the battle of Doiran against the Bulgarians in Macedonia on 18th September 1918. The regiment was represented in most of the major actions in Europe and North Africa during the Second World War, the 4th Battalion having some of its members massacred by German *Schutzstaffel* (SS) troops at Wornhout on 27th–28th May 1940 during the retreat to Dunkirk. The 7th Battalion earned the nickname 'the Globe Trotters' for service in France. Iraq, India and Italy. Since 1945 it has seen active service during the Malayan Emergency (1948–60), in Northern Ireland and in Bosnia in 1992–3.

VICTORIA CROSSES

First World War (2). Both are in the Regimental Museum.

NICKNAMES

The Two Twos: from the regimental number.

The Peep-o-Day Boys: presumably from service in aid of the civil power in

Ireland in the 1820s, the original 'Peep-o-Day Boys' being armed gangs of Orangemen in the 1790s.

The Red Knights: from the tradition of being clothed entirely in red while at Portsmouth in the 1790s.

The Lightning Conductors: from the 2nd Battalion being struck by lightning in South Africa in 1899.

BADGE

Traditionally, the Acorn and Oak-leaf badge is said to have been won at Dettingen on 27th June 1743. The regiment guarded King George II during one French attack and the monarch supposedly plucked a leaf from the tree by which he was standing and awarded it as a badge of honour. Since the regiment was in the Mediterranean at the time of Dettingen, an alternative suggestion is that a sprig of acorn appeared on the arms of the Duke of Norfolk.

CUSTOMS

In the presence of royalty and on other special occasions, wreaths of oak-leaves are carried on the Colours and the oak-leaf is worn in the head-dress, a tradition authorised by King George V in 1933.

FACINGS

Buff.

REGIMENTAL MARCHES

'Wha Wadna Fecht for Charlie' (quick step).
'The Miller of the Dee' (assembly march).
'Slow March 1772' (slow march).

COLOURS

Chester Cathedral; Chester Town Hall; Regimental Museum.

MEMORIALS

Chester Cathedral.

BATTLE HONOURS

Louisburg, Martinique 1762, Havannah, Meeanee, Hyderabad, Scinde, South Africa 1900–02.

Mons, Ypres 1914 '15 '18, Somme 1916 '18, Arras 1917 '18, Messines 1917 '18, Bapaume 1918, Doiran 1917 '18, Suvla, Gaza, Kut al Amara 1917.

St Omer-La Bassée, Normandy Landing, Capture of Tobruk, El Alamein, Mareth, Sicily 1943, Salerno, Rome, Gothic Line, Malta 1941–2.

LATER LINEAGE

The regiment has survived post-1945 reductions and amalgamations unscathed.

MUSEUMS

Cheshire Military Museum, The Castle, Chester CH1 2DN (telephone: 01244 327617; website: www.chester.ac.uk/militarymuseum).

CORNWALL

The Duke of Cornwall's Light Infantry (DCLI)
(32nd and 46th Foot)

ORIGINS AND DEVELOPMENT

The 32nd was raised in 1702 as Fox's Marines, while the 46th was raised in 1741 as Price's Regiment. In 1782 the 32nd was affiliated to Cornwall and the 46th to South Devonshire. In 1858 the 32nd was designated as a light infantry regiment to commemorate its defence of Lucknow during the 140 days of the Indian Mutiny siege in the previous year, for eighty-seven days of which the regiment was alone. In 1881 the regiments were linked as the 1st and 2nd Battalions, The Duke of Cornwall's Light Infantry. Reduced to a single battalion in 1948. Amalgamated 1959.

HISTORY

The first action of the 32nd was as marines during the seizure of a Spanish treasure fleet in Vigo Bay on 22nd October 1702. It then took part in the capture of Gibraltar two years later and in various amphibious operations along the Spanish coast. The 46th (then numbered the 57th) Foot was part of Sir John Cope's small force defeated by the Jacobites at Prestonpans on 20th September 1745, the battle being recalled in a popular contemporary Scottish song, 'Hey Johnnie Cope'. As the 46th, it saw service in North America during both the Seven Years War and the American War of Independence before being despatched to the West Indies in 1794. The 32nd was also in the West Indies in the 1790s but, then, during the Napoleonic

Wars, it served in the Peninsular War. At Waterloo on 18th June 1815, the French almost succeeded in taking its King's Colour during the struggle in which the divisional commander, Sir Thomas Picton, was killed. The 32nd fought in the Second Sikh War as well as in the Mutiny, while the 46th was in the Crimea. Not surprisingly, the date of the final relief of Lucknow (17th November) became the Regimental Day of the 32nd after its epic defence of the Residency under the command of Lieutenant Colonel (later Major-General Sir) John Inglis. Among the mementoes of Lucknow there is a fine portrait of Inglis and the 'Lucknow Tureen', dented by

'A private of Fox's Marines' by Charles Stadden.

During the Battle of Waterloo a French officer attempted to seize the King's Colour of the 32nd but was run through by Sergeant Switzer's pike and Ensign Birtwhistle's sword.

shot during the siege. The 2nd Battalion, which had served in Egypt in 1882, celebrated Paardeburg (18th February 1900), marking the surrender of the main Boer field army to Lord Roberts in the South African War. In the First World War, the 2nd Battalion reverted to the original role of the 32nd by being temporarily embarked as marines at Hong Kong. In the Second World War, the 1st Battalion suffered heavy losses against the Afrika Korps in Libya in early 1941. The 5th Battalion was heavily engaged in the fighting to break out from the Normandy beaches in June 1944, especially at Hill 112, known thereafter as Cornwall Hill. Subsequently, it was part of the force attempting to break through to Arnhem in September 1944.

VICTORIA CROSSES
   Indian Mutiny (4); Somaliland (2); First World War (1); Korean War (1). All eight are displayed in the Regimental Museum.

NICKNAMES
   The Red Feathers (46th): from Paoli (see below).
   The Docs: from 'Duke of Cornwall'.

BADGE
   As with other light infantry regiments, the badge was a light infantry Bugle, in this case surmounted by the Prince of Wales's Coronet, the Prince being the Duke of Cornwall. The role of the 46th in the successful attack on American rebels at Paoli on 21st September 1777 led them (like the 49th Foot) to dye their hat feathers red so that they would not be mistaken for others when the Americans vowed revenge. As a result, the bugle badge of the DCLI was always backed by red cloth.

MOTTO
   One and All: from that of the county of Cornwall.

CUSTOMS

The Loyal Toast was drunk only once a year in the officers' mess. This was on the sovereign's birthday and commemorated the shortage of wine during the siege of Lucknow.

FACINGS

White.

REGIMENTAL MARCHES

A combination of 'One and All' and 'Trelawny'.

COLOURS

St Petroc's Church, Bodmin.

MEMORIALS

The Barracks, Bodmin; Gruisbank Cemetery, Paardeburg, Orange Free State, South Africa (2nd Battalion); Baillie Guard, Lucknow, India.

BATTLE HONOURS

Gibraltar 1704–5, Dettingen, St Lucia 1778, Dominica, Rolica, Vimiera, Corunna, Salamanca, Pyrenees, Nivelle, Nive, Orthes, Peninsula, Waterloo, Mooltjan, Goojerat, Punjaub, Sevastopol, Lucknow, Tel-el-Kebir, Egypt 1882, Nile 1884–5, Paardeburg, South Africa 1899–1902.

Mons, Marne 1914, Ypres 1915–17, Somme 1916–18, Arras 1917, Passchendaele, Cambrai 1917–18, Sambre, Doiran 1917–18, Gaza.

Hill 112, Mont Pincon, Nederrijn, Geilenkirchen, Rhineland, North West Europe 1940, 1944–5, Gazala, Medjez Plain, Cassino II, Incentro.

LATER LINEAGE

The DCLI was amalgamated with The Somerset Light Infantry in 1959 as The Somerset and Cornwall Light Infantry. In 1968 this became, in turn, the 1st Battalion, The Light Infantry, a four-battalion regiment subsequently reduced to three battalions in 1969, and to two in 1993.

MUSEUMS

The Regimental Museum, The Duke of Cornwall's Light Infantry, The Keep, Bodmin, Cornwall PL31 1EG (telephone and fax: 01208 72810).

CUMBERLAND

The Border Regiment
(34th and 55th Foot)

ORIGINS AND DEVELOPMENT

The 34th was raised in Essex and Norfolk in 1702 as Lucas's Regiment while the 55th was raised at Stirling in 1757. In 1782 the 34th was linked with Cumberland and the 55th with Westmorland. In 1881 the two were linked as the 1st and 2nd Battalions, The Border Regiment. Reduced to a single battalion in 1950. Amalgamated 1959.

HISTORY

The 34th's first role was to garrison Landguard Fort at Sheerness and the Tower of London, but Carlisle Castle became its depot in the following year. The regiment led the Duke of Marlborough's assault on the fortress of Dousy in April 1710 and was present at both Fontenoy on 11th May 1745 and Culloden on 16th April 1746. The 55th suffered heavy losses in a failed assault on the French Fort Ticonderoga in North America on 8th July 1758. Returning to North America in 1775, the 55th served with Lord Howe's army in New York while the 34th were with Sir John Burgoyne's army, forced to surrender at Saratoga in October 1777. In the French Revolutionary and Napoleonic Wars, the 55th was again compelled to surrender, at St Lucia in October 1795, but the reconstituted battalion had its revenge by being part of the force that recaptured the island. At Bergen op Zoom on 8th March 1814 the 55th was once again captured by the French, although the Colours were successfully concealed by the Ensigns. Both regiments were in the Crimea and the 34th was then rushed to India in 1857. The 1st Battalion was in Burma suppressing dacoits (bandits) in 1889, while the 2nd Battalion was involved in operations on the North West Frontier in 1897. In the First World War, the 1st Battalion landed at Gallipoli on 25th April 1915, while the 11th (Lonsdale) Battalion was raised entirely at the expense of Lord Lonsdale, wearing his family's griffin badge. Both battalions served with the Shanghai Defence Force in 1927. During the Second World War, the 1st Battalion was converted to a glider-borne role, taking part in the first major British glider assault in Sicily on 9th–10th July 1943 and the doomed operation at Arnhem in September 1944. Three battalions served in Burma, the 4th in the second Chindit expedition behind Japanese lines between March and May 1944.

VICTORIA CROSSES

Crimean War (4); Indian Mutiny (1); First World War (5). Of these, four are in the Regimental Museum.

NICKNAMES

The Two Fives (55th): from the regimental number.

The Cattle Reeves: from the reivers (cattle thieves) on the Anglo-Scottish border in the Middle Ages.

BADGE

The China Dragon at the centre of the garter, superimposed on the Maltese Cross and backed by an eight-pointed Star, was awarded to the 55th for its service during the First China War of 1840–2, Lieutenant Butler capturing a Chinese Imperial

Dragon standard at Chusan.

MOTTO
Honi soit qui mal y pense ('Let him who thinks evil of it be ashamed').

CUSTOMS
Following the gallantry of the 34th at Fontenoy in 1745 a laurel wreath was placed on the Colours, and thereafter this image was emblazoned on the Colours. At Arroyo dos Molinos on 28th October 1811 during the Peninsular War, the 2/34th captured the drums of the French 34th Infantry Regiment. Subsequently, the captured drums were paraded annually on Arroyo Day to commemorate the event. As a result of the performance of the 1st Battalion in the assault on Sicily, King George VI granted the right to wear a glider badge on the right sleeve.

FACINGS
Yellow.

REGIMENTAL MARCHES
'John Peel'.
'Lass O'Gowrie'.
'Horn of the Hunter' (slow march).

COLOURS
Carlisle Cathedral.

MEMORIALS
Carlisle Cathedral.

BATTLE HONOURS
Havannah, St Lucia 1778, Albuhera, Arroyo dos Molinos, Vittoria, Pyrenees, Nivelle, Nive, Orthes, Peninsula, Alma, Inkerman, Sevastopol, Lucknow, Relief of Ladysmith, South Africa 1899–1902, Afghanistan 1919.

Ypres 1914 '15 '17 '18, Langemarck 1914 '17, Somme 1916 '18, Arras 1917 '18, Cambrai 1917 '18, Lys, France and Flanders 1914–18, Vittorio Veneto, Macedonia 1915–18, Gallipoli 1915–16.

Dunkirk 1940, Arnhem 1944, North West Europe 1940 '44, Tobruk 1941, Landing in Sicily, Imphal, Myinmu Bridgehead, Meiktila, Chindits 1944, Burma 1943–5.

LATER LINEAGE
Amalgamated 1959 with The King's Own Royal Regiment (Lancaster) as The King's Own Royal Border Regiment.

MUSEUMS
The Museum of The Border Regiment and The King's Own Royal Border Regiment, Queen Mary's Tower, Carlisle Castle, Carlisle, Cumbria CA3 8UR (telephone: 01228 532774; website: www.army.mod.uk/ceremonialandheritage/museums).

DERBYSHIRE
(see **Nottinghamshire**)

DEVON

THE DEVONSHIRE REGIMENT
(11th Foot)

ORIGINS AND DEVELOPMENT

The 11th Foot was raised at Bristol in 1685 as the Duke of Beaufort's Regiment. In 1782 it was affiliated to north Devonshire and in 1881 became the Devonshire Regiment. A 2nd Battalion existed from 1858 to 1948. Amalgamated 1958.

HISTORY

Soon after being raised, the 11th went to Ireland, being present at the battle of the Boyne on 1st July 1690. During the War of Spanish Succession it served in Spain and Portugal, distinguishing itself at Almanza on 25th April 1707. Subsequently, it was present at the reverse suffered against the Jacobites at Sheriffmuir on 13th November 1715, while it also fought at both Dettingen on 16th June 1743 and Fontenoy on 30th April 1745. The 11th joined Wellington's army in the Peninsula in 1809, taking heavy losses at Salamanca on 22nd July 1812 in an attack against a French division. In 1827 it served in Portugal again during the brief British intervention on behalf of Queen Doña Maria against her reactionary uncle Dom Miguel, while its garrison service included an eight-year tour from 1828 of the Ionian islands, then under British protection. The 2/11th, formed in 1858, became the first British regiment to march through the Bolan Pass in the hot-weather period in July 1880 during the Second Afghan War. The 1st Battalion was caught in Ladysmith in October 1899 and distinguished itself particularly during the failed Boer attempt to seize the commanding Wagon Hill on 6th January 1900. Meanwhile, the 2nd Battalion was part of the relieving force, engaged at Colenso, Spion Kop and Vaal Krantz. In the First World War, the 2nd Battalion won the French Croix de Guerre by holding the Bois des Buttes almost literally to the last man on 27th May 1918 during the major German offensive towards Paris. Earlier, at Mansel Copse near Mametz on the Somme, a famous sign – 'The Devons held this trench, the Devons hold it still' – was displayed for many years at the entrance to the Devonshire Cemetery. Before the Second World War, the 2nd Battalion had been stationed in Malta. As well as holding responsibility for defence against possible invasion, the battalion also helped keep the Royal Air Force's runways in repair during the Italian and German aerial bombardment of the island which began in June 1940.

VICTORIA CROSSES

South African War (1); First World War (2). All are displayed in the Regimental Museum.

NICKNAMES

The Bloody Eleventh: from the losses suffered at Salamanca on 22nd July 1812, amounting to sixteen officers and 325 other ranks killed or wounded out of 412 men who went into action.

BADGE

The Castle, in a circle on an eight-pointed Star, is that of Exeter.

MOTTO

Semper fidelis ('Ever faithful').

'The Devons crossing the Tugela on their way to Spion Kop'. Based upon a photograph by R. Darley taken during the South African War.

FACINGS
Lincoln green.

REGIMENTAL MARCHES
'We've Lived and Loved Together'.
'Widecombe Fair'.
'The Rose of Devon' (slow march).

COLOURS
Exeter Cathedral.

MEMORIALS
Exeter Cathedral; Wagon Hill and Town Centre, Ladysmith, KwaZulu-Natal, South Africa (1st Battalion); Colenso, KwaZulu-Natal, South Africa (2nd Battalion); Plymouth Hoe (South African War); Devonshire Cemetery, Mametz, Somme, France (9th Battalion); Bois de Buttes, Ville-aux-Bois (2nd Battalion); Regalbuto, Sicily (2nd Battalion, 1943); St Peter-upon-Cornhill Church, London.

BATTLE HONOURS
Dettingen, Salamanca, Pyrenees, Nivelle, Nive, Orthes, Toulouse, Peninsula, Afghanistan 1879–80, Tirah, Defence of Ladysmith, South Africa 1899–1902.
La Bassée 1914, Ypres 1915 '17, Loos, Somme 1916 '18, Bois des Buttes, Hindenburg Line, Vittorio Veneto, Doiran 1917 '18, Palestine 1917 '18, Mesopotamia 1916 '18.
Normandy Landing, Caen, Rhine, North West Europe 1944 '45, Landing in Sicily, Regalbuto, Malta 1940 '42, Imphal, Myinmu Bridgehead, Burma 1943 '45.

LATER LINEAGE
Amalgamated in 1958 with The Dorset Regiment as The Devonshire and Dorset Regiment.

MUSEUMS
The Keep Military Museum, The Keep, Bridport Road, Dorchester, Dorset DT1 1RN (telephone: 01305 264066; fax: 01305 250373; website: www.keepmilitarymuseum.org). Additional items are displayed in *St Nicholas Priory*, The Mint, Fore Street, Exeter EX1 1JN (telephone: 01392 665858; website: www.exeter.gov.uk); *Torquay Museum*, 529 Babbacombe Road, Torquay TQ1 1HG (telephone: 01803 293975; website: www.torquaymuseum.org); *The Museum of North Devon*, The Square, Barnstaple, Devon EX32 8LN (telephone: 01271 346747; website: www.army.mod.uk/ceremonialandheritage/museums); and *Crown Hill Fort*, Crownhill Fort Road, Plymouth, Devon PL6 5BX (telephone: 01752 793754; website: www.crownhillfort.co.uk).

DORSET

The Dorset Regiment
(39th and 54th Foot)

ORIGINS AND DEVELOPMENT

The 39th was raised in 1702 as Coote's Regiment, while the 54th was raised in 1755 (originally as the 56th but renumbered in 1757). In 1782 the 54th was affiliated to West Norfolk while the 39th was affiliated to Dorset in 1807. In 1881 the regiments were linked as the 1st and 2nd Battalions, The Dorset Regiment. Reduced to a single battalion in 1948. Amalgamated 1958.

HISTORY

The 39th initially experienced much garrison service in Ireland and the West Indies, before being the first King's regiment sent to India. It contributed greatly to the victory at Plassey on 23rd June 1757, in which Robert Clive's small force of about three thousand Europeans and native troops defeated some fifty thousand men of the Nabob of Bengal's army, thus laying the foundations of British India. Later the regiment served throughout the whole four-year siege of Gibraltar by the Spanish and French between 1779 and 1783. Just as Plassey was a unique battle honour for the 39th, so Marabout was a unique battle honour for the 54th, which captured this fort guarding the harbour of Alexandria on 21st August 1801 during

the British campaign to eject the French from Egypt. The 'Marabout Gun' was captured by the 54th at Alexandria and was paraded regularly with the regiment until 1840, when the privilege was withdrawn and the battle honour 'Marabout' awarded instead. A notable member of the 54th was the later radical political polemicist William Cobbett, who retired as sergeant major in 1790. Officers of the 39th undertook much of the exploration of New South Wales while the regiment was guarding convict settlements in Australia between 1825 and 1832. On 20th October 1897 the 1st Battalion took part in the successful storming of the heights

Men of the 1st Dorsets manning 38 Trench at Hill 60 in the spring of 1915. The soldier seated in the middle is holding a makeshift periscope. It was opposite these trenches, on 1st May 1915, that the Germans launched a devastating gas attack.

33

of Dargai in the Tirah during the worst tribal uprising faced by the British on the North West Frontier. Six battalions saw active service overseas during the First World War, the 1st Battalion distinguishing itself at La Bassée during the First Battle of Ypres in October 1914. The 2nd Battalion was in Mesopotamia, falling into Turkish hands at the capture of Kut in April 1916: of 350 men captured, only seventy survived. During the Second World War, the 1st Battalion was part of the Malta garrison and, later, one of the first two British battalions to land in Normandy, on 6th June 1944. The 4th and 5th Battalions took part in the advance from Normandy to the Rhine by the celebrated 43rd (Wessex) Division.

VICTORIA CROSSES
Tirah, 1897 (1). Displayed in the Regimental Museum.

NICKNAMES
Sankey's Horse (39th): from Almanza on 27th April 1707, when Colonel Sankey was so anxious to reach the battle that he mounted his men on mules.
The Flamers (54th): from an incident in 1781 when the regiment burned twelve American privateers anchored at New London in Connecticut.

BADGE
The Castle and Key – the arms granted to Gibraltar by King Ferdinand II of Spain in 1502 – were a reminder of the 39th Foot's part in the defence of the Rock, while the motto *Primus in Indis* ('First in India') commemorated the fact that the 39th was the first British regiment to serve in India. The Sphinx and 'Marabout' derived from the 54th's service in Egypt in 1801.

MOTTOES
Primus in Indis ('First in India').
Montis insignia Calpe ('The insignia of Gibraltar is the Rock' – from the Moorish name of Gibraltar as 'Mount Calpe').

The Colours of The Dorset Regiment in Sherborne Abbey church.

34

CUSTOMS

The 54th and, later, the Dorsets, celebrated Sarah Sands Day annually in November in memory of the men saving the troopship *Sarah Sands* from explosion off Mauritius on 11th November 1857. They threw the powder kegs overboard after a fire started in the hold and the crew abandoned the regiment and its families.

FACINGS

Green.

REGIMENTAL MARCHES

'The Maid of Glenconnel'.

'The Farmer's Boy'.

COLOURS

Sherborne Abbey.

MEMORIALS

Borough Gardens, Dorchester (Tirah); Dorset County Hospital, Dorchester (First World War). Memorial houses in Dorchester, Sherborne and Upton.

BATTLE HONOURS

Plassey, Martinique, Marabout, Albuhera, Vittoria, Pyrenees, Nivelle, Nive, Orthes, Peninsula, Ava, Maharajpore, Sevastopol, Tirah, Relief of Ladysmith, South Africa 1899–1902.

Mons, Marne, Ypres 1915 '17, Khan Baghdadi, Hindenburg Line, Sambre, Suvla, Gaza, Shaiba, Ctesiphon.

St Omer-La Bassée, Normandy Landing, Caen, Arnhem 1944, Aam, Geilenkirchen, Landing in Sicily, Malta 1940–2, Kohima, Mandalay.

LATER LINEAGE

Amalgamated in 1958 with The Devonshire Regiment as The Devonshire and Dorset Regiment.

MUSEUMS

The Keep Military Museum, The Keep, Bridport Road, Dorchester, Dorset DT1 1RN (telephone: 01305 264066; fax: 01305 250373; website: www.keepmilitarymuseum.org).

DURHAM

The Durham Light Infantry (DLI)
(68th and 106th Foot)

ORIGINS AND DEVELOPMENT

The 68th was raised in May 1758 from the 2/23rd Foot. In 1782 it was affiliated to Durham, and in 1808 converted to a light infantry role. The 106th was originally the 2nd Bombay European Infantry raised by the East India Company in 1839 and converted to a light infantry role in 1840. Following the abolition of the Company in 1858, its European regiments were brought on to the British establishment with the 2nd Bombay European Light Infantry redesignated the 106th Foot in 1862. The two regiments were linked in 1881 as the 1st and 2nd Battalions, The Durham Light Infantry. The two battalions were amalgamated in 1948 although the 2nd Battalion was then briefly revived between 1952 and 1955. In 1968 the regiment became the 4th Battalion, The Light Infantry.

HISTORY

The link of the 68th with Durham was forged early, its first colonel, John Lambton, being from an established county family and, indeed, grandfather of the first Earl of Durham. The leather infantryman's cap, known as the 'Lambton Cap', is a controversial relic. Though it bears the title 'Faithful', the monogram 'JL' and the Lambton family Lamb's Head crest, a Royal Warrant in 1751 had forbidden colonels to place their family arms on any regimental equipment. In 1808 it became the third regiment to be converted to light infantry, following that of the 43rd and 52nd, and it saw service at Walcheren in 1809. Arriving in the Peninsula in 1811, it took part in Wellington's later victories. In action against the Maoris at the Gate Pa in New Zealand on 29th April 1864, Sergeant John Murray won the Victoria Cross

*The Lambton Cap,
68th Foot, c.1770.*

(VC) for saving the life of Corporal John Byrne, who had won the regiment's first VC at Inkerman in the Crimea. The 106th was one of the later creations of the East India Company, seeing service in the Persian War of 1856–7. The first action of the new DLI was also the last in which the British army wore red coats, at Ginnis in the Sudan on 30th December 1885 – though, ironically, the 2nd Battalion was actually in khaki. A total of thirty-seven regular, Territorial and service battalions of the DLI served in the First World War. Lieutenant Colonel Roland Boys 'Boy' Bradford, VC, MC, killed at Cambrai in November 1917, was the youngest brigade commander in the army at the time of his death. There was particularly fierce fighting on the Somme for control of the feature known as the 'Butte de Warlencourt', which reputedly changed hands seventeen times in the course of the Somme campaign between July and November 1916. Upon its final capture in February 1917, the 6th, 8th and 9th Battalions each set up a memorial cross with an additional cross for 151 Brigade, in which all served. All were subsequently removed but the brigade cross is now displayed in Durham Cathedral. A Second World War relic is the two-pounder gun crewed by Private Adam Wakenshaw of the 9th Battalion at Mersa Matruh in North Africa in June 1942, when he won a posthumous Victoria Cross (also on display) for silencing a German gun menacing the battalion's rearguard when he had already lost his left arm. Arriving in Korea in September 1952, the 1st Battalion was responsible for the defence of the key sectors of Point 355 and the Hook during the last stages of the protracted negotiations leading to the armistice in June 1953. The battalion also saw service at Suez in 1956, in Cyprus, and in Borneo in 1966 during the Confrontation between Indonesia and Malaysia (1962–6).

VICTORIA CROSSES
Crimean War (2); Third Maori War (1); First World War (6); Second World War (2). Of these, seven are displayed in the Regimental Museum.

NICKNAMES
The Faithful Durhams: from service against the Caribs at St Vincent in the West Indies in 1772. Though dropped in 1780, the title persisted as a nickname.

BADGE
A light infantry Bugle with 'DLI' on its strings.

MOTTO
Honi soit qui mal y pense ('Let him who thinks evil of it be ashamed').

CUSTOMS
Inkerman Day (5th November) was celebrated annually. The 68th was said to be the only regiment to have fought in red since it alone supposedly discarded its greatcoats in this winter battle. The 2nd Battalion celebrated Hooge Day (9th August) annually, in memory of a 1915 action outside Ypres.

FACINGS
Dark green.

REGIMENTAL MARCHES
'The Light Barque' (quick march).
'The Old 68th' (slow march).
'The Keel Row and Moneymusk' (double march).

1st Battalion, The Durham Light Infantry in Korea, 1952–3.

COLOURS
Durham Cathedral; Parish Church, Barnard Castle.

MEMORIALS
Memorial Gardens, Durham Cathedral Close.

BATTLE HONOURS
Salamanca, Vittoria, Pyrenees, Nivelle, Orthes, Peninsula, Alma, Inkerman, Sevastopol, Reshire, Bushire, Koosh-ab, Persia, New Zealand, Relief of Ladysmith, South Africa 1899–1902.

Aisne 1914 '18, Ypres 1915 '17 '18, Hooge 1915, Loos, Somme 1916 '18, Arras 1917 '18, Messines 1917, Lys, Hindenburg Line, Sambre.

Dunkirk 1940, Tilly-sur-Seulles, Defence of Rauray, Gheel, Tobruk 1941, El Alamein, Mareth, Primosole Bridge, Salerno, Kohima, Korea 1952–3.

LATER LINEAGE
4th Battalion, The Light Infantry was disbanded in March 1969.

MUSEUMS
The Durham Light Infantry Museum and Durham Art Gallery, Aykley Heads, Durham DH1 5TU (telephone: 0191 384 2214; website: www.durham.gov.uk).

ESSEX

The Essex Regiment
(44th and 56th Foot)

ORIGINS AND DEVELOPMENT

The 44th was raised in 1741 and the 56th was raised in 1755. In 1782 the two were affiliated respectively with east Essex and west Essex. In 1881 they were linked as the 1st and 2nd Battalions, The Essex Regiment. Reduced to a single battalion in 1948. Amalgamated 1959.

HISTORY

The 44th saw its first action at Prestonpans on 20th September 1745, its commanding officer and twelve other officers being captured by the Jacobites. The 44th then had the misfortune to participate in another defeat in July 1755, this time the ambush of Major-General Edward Braddock's force on the Monongahela by the French and their Indian allies in North America. The 56th began its active service as part of the expedition to Havana in 1762 and was part of the Gibraltar garrison during the great siege from 1779 to 1783, returning to the West Indies in 1795. The 44th took part in the expedition to Egypt in 1801 and in various amphibious operations in the Mediterranean, before again returning to North America for the Anglo-American War (1812–14), suffering heavy losses at New Orleans on 8th January 1815. The 2/44th served in the Peninsula as well as in the Waterloo campaign. Indeed, at Quatre Bras on 16th June 1815 the wounded ensign James Christie flung himself over the Regimental Colour to prevent it being captured by a French lancer. The Frenchman got away with a small piece torn from beneath Christie's body, but other men of the regiment pursed the lancer and retrieved the piece. The 44th went to India in 1823 and was the only British regiment with the force compelled to retreat from Kabul back to India in 1841. Just fifty or so survivors from an army of some 4500 fighting men – nearly all from the 44th – made a last stand at Gandamak on 13th January 1842, Lieutenant Souter wrapping the Regimental Colour around his body to prevent it being captured. Together with four others Souter was captured and survived, and he kept the Colour hidden until released from captivity. In the First World War the 1st Battalion landed at W Beach, Gallipoli, on 25th April 1915, moving to the Western Front in 1916 and serving in the Anglo-Irish War (1919–20). The 2nd Battalion was engaged at Le Cateau on 26th August 1914 and remained on the Western Front throughout. During the Second World War, the 1st Battalion saw service in Italian East Africa, Iraq and Syria before going to Burma in 1943. The 2nd Battalion, meanwhile, took part in both the Dunkirk and Normandy campaigns. The 1/4th, 1/5th and 2/5th all saw service in the Middle East.

VICTORIA CROSSES

Crimean War (1); Second China War (2); South African War (1); First World War (1); Second World War (1). Of these, four are in the Regimental Museum.

NICKNAMES

The Pompadours (56th): from the original 'Pompadour' purple facings, purple being a colour made fashionable in the eighteenth century by the mistress of the French king Louis XIV, Madame de Pompadour.

The Fighting Fours: from the regimental number.

BADGE

The Castle and Key were awarded to the 56th for the defence of Gibraltar, while the Sphinx was won by the 44th for service in Egypt in 1801.

MOTTO

Montis insignia Calpe ('The insignia of Gibraltar is the Rock').

CUSTOMS

The 44th having captured the eagle of the French 62nd Regiment at Salamanca on 22nd July 1812, the officer's collar badge of the Essex Regiment was an eagle, and an eagle also appeared on the buttons of the regiment. On St Patrick's Day the regiment's Corps of Drums used to beat reveille by playing Irish airs, marking the existence of the 2/44th, which had captured the eagle, between its raising in 1803 and its disbandment in 1815.

FACINGS

White.

REGIMENTAL MARCHES

'The Hampshires' (2nd Battalion).
'We'll gang nae mair to yon toun' (1st Battalion).

COLOURS

Regimental Museum, Chelmsford; Parish Church of Colchester; Chelmsford Cathedral; Garrison Church, Warley, Brentwood.

MEMORIALS

Garrison Church, Warley, Brentwood; Bell Meadow, Chelmsford Cathedral.

BATTLE HONOURS

Moro, Havannah, Badajoz, Salamanca, Peninsula, Bladensburg, Waterloo, Ava, Alma, Inkerman, Sevastopol, Taku Forts, Nile 1884–5, Relief of Kimberley, Paardeburg, South Africa 1899–1902.

Le Cateau, Marne 1914, Ypres 1915 '17, Loos, Somme 1916 '18, Arras 1917 '18, Cambrai 1917, Selle, Gallipoli 1915–16, Gaza.

Zetten, North West Europe 1940 '1944–5, Palmyra, Tobruk 1941, Defence of Alamein Line, Enfidaville, Sangro, Villa Grande, Cassino I, Chindits 1944.

LATER LINEAGE

Amalgamated in 1959 with The Bedfordshire and Hertfordshire Regiment as the 3rd East Anglian Regiment. In 1964 it became the 3rd Battalion, The Royal Anglian Regiment, a four-battalion regiment reduced to three battalions in 1970 and to two in 1992.

MUSEUMS

The Essex Regiment Museum, Oaklands Park, Moulsham Street, Chelmsford, Essex CM2 9AQ (telephone: 01245 615100; website: www.army.mod.uk/ceremonialandheritage/museums).

GLOUCESTERSHIRE

The Gloucestershire Regiment
(28th and 61st Foot)

ORIGINS AND DEVELOPMENT

The 28th Foot was raised in 1694 as Gibson's Regiment, while the 61st was raised in 1756 from the 2/3rd Foot. In 1782 they were affiliated respectively to north and south Gloucestershire. In 1881 they became the 1st and 2nd Battalions, The Gloucestershire Regiment. Reduced to a single battalion in 1948. Amalgamated 1994.

HISTORY

The 28th was sent to Newfoundland in 1697 to restore a colony all but destroyed by the French. It won its first battle honour in Marlborough's victory at Ramillies on 18th July 1705, subsequently suffering heavy losses at Almanza in Spain on 27th April 1707. The 28th was also present at both Fontenoy in 1745 and Quebec in 1757. The 28th's best-known feat came at Alexandria on 21st March 1801 when it was attacked in both the front and the rear simultaneously: the commanding officer ordered the rear rank to 'right about face' and the French were successfully beaten off. The 28th also fought in Wellington's delaying action at Quatre Bras on 16th June 1815, two days before Waterloo, being immortalised in a famous painting by the Victorian battle artist Lady Butler. The 61st took part in the 'Waterloo of India', the costly victory over the Sikhs at Chillianwallah on 13th January 1849. At Sari Bair (also known as 'Chunuk Bair') on Gallipoli on 6th August 1915 every officer and senior non-commissioned officer of the 7th Battalion was either killed or wounded but the men kept fighting throughout the day. Such gallantry was again famously

Second Lieutenant David Holdsworth, Captain M. G. Harvey and Lieutenant Denys Whatmore at a rest camp after leading their men of The Gloucestershire Regiment back from the Battle of Imjin River in Korea, 22nd to 25th April 1951.

displayed when the 1st Battalion fought for four days to hold the United Nations line on Hill 235, overlooking the Imjin river, against the Chinese communists in Korea before being overwhelmed on 25th April 1951. Two Victoria Crosses were won, one posthumously to an officer attached from the Duke of Cornwall's Light Infantry, and the regiment received the American president's Distinguished Unit Citation. The regiment's medal collection includes the Victoria Cross won by its commanding officer at the Imjin, Lieutenant Colonel J. P. Carne. A Celtic cross carved by Carne while a prisoner in Chinese hands is in Gloucester Cathedral.

VICTORIA CROSSES

Indian Mutiny (1); First World War (5); Korean War (1). Of these, four are in the Regimental Museum.

NICKNAMES

The Slashers: from the 28th at the battle of White Plains on 28th October 1776, when the men used their sword bayonets to 'slash' through the long grass impeding their advance on the American rebels.

The Fore and Aft: from the back badge (see under Customs).

The Back Numbers: as above.

BADGE

The Sphinx and 'Egypt' on two twigs of laurel commemorates the action of the 28th at Alexandria in 1801. The 61st was also in Egypt and was also entitled to the sphinx badge.

MOTTO

Honi soit qui mal y pense ('Let him who thinks evil of it be ashamed').

'Soldiers of the 28th' by Thomas Hand, c.1803.

CUSTOMS

As a result of the action at Alexandria, the 28th was given the unique privilege of wearing its regimental number as a back badge as well as at the front of the head-dress. When the 28th and 61st were linked, both wore the back badge in the form of a sphinx encircled by a laurel wreath. Streamers were added to the Colours as a result of the award of the Presidential Citation for the Imjin in 1951. In the officer's mess, the usual procedure of the vice-president proposing the Loyal Toast by saying 'Gentlemen, the King [or Queen]' was varied by saying 'The King [or Queen], Mr President' since, after one engagement in the Peninsular War, only two officers remained unscathed and were present at dinner.

FACINGS

White.

REGIMENTAL MARCHES

'The Kinnegad Slashers' (28th).
'The Highland Piper' (61st).

COLOURS

The Regimental Museum.

MEMORIALS

Clifton, Bristol (South African War); Tchrengula and Town Centre, Ladysmith, KwaZulu-Natal, South Africa (1st Battalion); President Avenue, Bloemfontein, Orange Free State, South Africa (2nd Battalion); Clapham Junction, Menin Road, Ypres, Belgium (1st and 2nd Battalions, 1914–15).

BATTLE HONOURS

Ramillies, Louisburg, Guadaloupe 1759, Martinique 1762, Havannah, St Lucia 1778, Maida, Corunna, Talavera, Busaco, Barrosa, Albuhera, Salamanca, Vittoria, Pyrenees, Nivelle, Nive, Orthes, Toulouse, Peninsula, Waterloo, Chillianwallah, Goojerat, Punjaub, Alma, Inkerman, Sevastopol, Delhi 1857, Defence of Ladysmith, Relief of Kimberley, Paardeburg, South Africa 1899–1902.

Mons, Ypres 1914 '15 '17, Loos, Somme 1916 '18, Lys, Selle, Vittorio Veneto, Doiran 1917, Sari Bair, Baghdad.

Defence of Escaut, Cassel, Mont Pincon, Falaise, North West Europe 1940 '1944–5, Taukyan, Paungde, Pinwe, Myitson, Burma 1942 '44–5, Imjin, Korea 1950–1.

LATER LINEAGE

Amalgamated in 1994 with The Duke of Edinburgh's Royal Regiment as The Royal Gloucestershire, Berkshire and Wiltshire Regiment.

MUSEUMS

Soldiers of Gloucestershire Museum, Custom House, Gloucester Docks, Gloucester GL1 2HE (telephone: 01452 522682; fax: 01452 311116; website: www.glosters.org.uk).

HAMPSHIRE

The Royal Hampshire Regiment
(37th and 67th Foot)

ORIGINS AND DEVELOPMENT

The 37th was raised in Ireland in 1702 as Meredith's Regiment while the 67th was raised in 1758 from the 2/20th Foot. In 1782 they were affiliated respectively with north and south Hampshire, becoming in 1881 the 1st and 2nd Battalions, The Hampshire Regiment. The title of Royal Hampshire Regiment was granted in 1946 in recognition of its service in the Second World War, the regiment being reduced to a single battalion in 1948. Having become a single company in 1970, the battalion was reformed two years later. Amalgamated 1992.

HISTORY

The 37th arrived in Flanders in 1703, taking part in all four of Marlborough's victories at Blenheim, Ramillies, Oudenarde and Malplaquet. Subsequently, the regiment was at Dettingen on 27th June 1743 before being sent back to Britain to confront the Jacobite rebellion. At Minden on 1st August 1759 six British (and three Hanoverian) regiments including the 37th advanced and routed a large force of French cavalry and infantry through a mistaken order. After the battle, they decked their hats with roses. The 67th's first colonel was James Wolfe, later killed at Quebec, but the regiment never served under his command, its first action being the amphibious assault on St Malo in 1758. Garrison service followed until the 1/67th went to India in 1805, participating in the Maratha campaigns during twenty-one long years in India until 1826. Having seen service during the American War of Independence, the 37th distinguished itself in the Duke of York's otherwise unsuccessful campaign in Flanders in 1794 but then went to the West Indies. Four members of the 67th won the Victoria Cross in the storming of the Taku Forts on 21st August 1860 during the Third China War, Ensign John Chaplin planting the Queen's Colour on the fort wall under heavy fire. On 25th April 1915 two companies of the 2nd Battalion landed on V Beach at Cape Helles, Gallipoli, together with supporting companies from the 1st Royal Dublin Fusiliers and the 1st Royal Munster Fusiliers, from the converted collier *River Clyde*. The collier grounded just short of the beach and, emerging from sally ports cut in its sides, the men came under such heavy fire that they were forced to remain on the ship until darkness. In all, fifty-six battle honours were won in the First World War. In 1939 the 2nd Battalion was the first to disembark in France as part of the British Expeditionary Force. Subsequently, the 2nd served in Tunisia (with particular distinction at the Battle of 'Tebourba Gap', November–December 1942) together with three Territorial battalions, 1st/4th, 2nd/4th and 5th Battalions. The 1st Battalion took part in the Siege of Malta, 1941–3, the Assault Landings in Sicily, 10th July 1943, and Italy, 8th September 1943, returning to the United Kingdom to land in Normandy on D-Day, 6th June 1944. Four battalions of the regiment had long and arduous operations in the Italian campaign. Post-war service by the 1st Battalion included operational tours in Palestine, 1946–7; Malaya, 1954–6; the Caribbean Area, Jamaica, British Honduras and British Guiana, 1960–2; Borneo, 1966; Cyprus, 1968; Hong Kong, 1975; the Falkland Islands and South Georgia, 1982; as well as eight operational tours in Northern Ireland.

Charles Dixon's painting of the landing from 'River Clyde' at Gallipoli in 1915.

VICTORIA CROSSES
Second China War (4); First World War (3); Second World War (3). Of these, seven are in the Regimental Museum.

NICKNAMES
The Tigers: from the badge.

BADGE
The Royal Bengal Tiger was awarded to the 67th in 1826 by King George IV for its service in India from 1805 to 1826. The Hampshire Rose is Henry V's 'Lancastrian' Rose, supposedly awarded by him to the trained bands of the County of Southampton who fought for him at Agincourt in 1415. Formerly worn in the authorised officer's cap badge of the Hampshire Militia until 1881, it was reauthorised for wear in the officer's cap badge and soldier's cap badge of The Hampshire Regiment in 1881. The Imperial Crown represents that of the Order of the Star of India.

CUSTOMS
As one of the six 'Minden' regiments, the 37th celebrated the anniversary of the battle by wearing a small single red rose in their head-dress, a custom maintained by all battalions of the regiment since 1881.

FACINGS
Yellow.

REGIMENTAL MARCHES
'The Highland Piper' (37th).
'We'll gang nae mair tae yon toun' (67th).
'Cork Hill' (3rd Militia Battalion).

COLOURS
The Regimental Museum; Winchester Cathedral; St Peter's Church, Bournemouth.

'Fritz', regimental mascot, a Pyrenean German army war dog which was captured by the 1st Battalion on the Normandy beaches, 'D' Day, 6th June 1944. After quarantine and 're-training', groomed and ceremonially dressed, and led by the Dog Major, he headed the marching contingents of the five 1945/46 County 'Freedom' Marches, bestowed on the regiment for service 1939–45.

MEMORIALS

Winchester Cathedral; All Saints Church, Aldershot; The Chapel, The Royal Military Academy, Sandhurst; Barberton and Ermelo, South Africa (2nd Battalion); St George's Church, Tunisia; Anglican Church, Naples.

BATTLE HONOURS

Blenheim, Ramillies, Oudenarde, Malplaquet, Dettingen, Belleisle, Tournay, Barrosa, Peninsula, Taku Forts, Pekin 1860, Charasia, Kabul 1879, Afghanistan 1878–80, Burma 1885–7, Paardeburg, South Africa 1900–02.

Retreat from Mons, Ypres 1915 '17 '18, Somme 1916 '18, Arras 1917 '18, Cambrai 1917 '18, Doiran 1917 '18, Landing at Helles, Suvla, Gaza, Kut al Amara 1915–18.

Dunkirk 1940, Normandy Landing, Caen, Rhine, Tebourba Gap, Hunt's Gap, Salerno, Cassino II, Gothic Line, Malta 1941–2.

LATER LINEAGE

Amalgamated in 1992 with The Queen's Regiment as The Princess of Wales's Royal Regiment (Queen's and Royal Hampshires).

MUSEUMS

The Royal Hampshire Regiment Museum, Serle's House, Southgate Street, Winchester, Hampshire SO23 9EG (telephone: 01962 863658).

HEREFORDSHIRE

The Herefordshire Light Infantry (TA)

ORIGINS AND DEVELOPMENT

Eight corps of rifle volunteers were raised in Herefordshire in 1860. The corps were brought together as the 1st Administrative Battalion, The Herefordshire Rifle Volunteers in February 1861 and consolidated as the 1st Herefordshire (Hereford and Radnor) Rifle Volunteer Corps in 1880. In 1881 it nominally became the 3rd Volunteer Battalion, King's Shropshire Light Infantry, but preferred to retain its own county volunteer title. In 1908 it became the 1st Battalion, The Herefordshire Battalion, The King's Shropshire Light Infantry and, shortly afterwards, 1st Battalion, The Herefordshire Regiment (TF). With the formation of the Territorial Army in 1920, it was originally proposed that the regiment should become a heavy artillery regiment. However, as a result of a huge outcry in the county it was reformed as infantry as The Herefordshire Regiment (TA), without the Radnorshire Companies. Thus the link with Radnorshire was finally broken. In 1947, in recognition of its war services, it became The Herefordshire Light Infantry. Amalgamated 1967.

HISTORY

During the South African War, two volunteer service companies were formed, drawn from all three volunteer battalions of The King's Shropshire Light Infantry. One joined the 2nd Battalion, The King's Shropshire Light Infantry in 1900. A second company went out in 1901. The motto, adopted in 1908 by permission of King Edward VII, was that of the Clan Mackay, of which the commanding officer, Lieutenant Colonel J. G. Scobie, was a member. In the First World War, the 1/1st Battalion served at Gallipoli with the 53rd (Welsh) Division. Its attack between Hetman Chair and Kaslar Chair at Suvla Bay on 9th August 1915 was pressed, according to General Sir Ian Hamilton's report, with 'impetuosity and courage'. The battalion was involved in the defence of Egypt and the Canal Zone at the battle of Rumani in July 1916. It then served in Palestine, taking part in all three battles of Gaza in March, April and October 1917, at Beersheba and Khuweilfeh and then at the battle of Tel Asur in March 1918, before transferring to the Western Front in June 1918, where it served with 34th Division. In the Second World War, the 1st Battalion served in 159th Infantry Brigade, first with 53rd (Welsh) Division and, later, with 11th Armoured Division as lorried infantry in the North West Europe campaign of 1944–5. It distinguished itself at Odon on 30th–31st July 1944 during Operation *Epsom*, one of the early attempts to break out from the Normandy bridgehead, as well as at Caumont on 30th–31st July in the final breakout, code-named Operation *Bluecoat*, and the battles around the Falaise pocket. It led the drive to Antwerp, fought on the Maas, and across the Rhine to Lubeck. It also took part in Operation *Blackout*, the rounding up of the members of the Supreme Command of the German Armed Forces (OKW) at Flensburg on 23rd May 1945, including Hitler's successor, Grand Admiral Doenitz. Indeed, the two pennants from Doenitz's staff car were secured by the regiment for safe keeping.

NICKNAMES

The Grasshoppers: from the green facings of the 36th Foot when affiliated to Herefordshire.

BADGE
Approved in 1950, the Lion of the Herefordshire Regiment stood within a Light Infantry bugle. Originally, the Lion was part of the arms of the City of Hereford.

MOTTO
Manu Forti ('With strong hand').

FACINGS
Grass green.

REGIMENTAL MARCHES
'The Lincolnshire Poacher' (from the regiment's link with 36th Foot, which recruited in Lincolnshire).
'To Be a Farmer's Boy'.

COLOURS
TA Centre, Harold Street, Hereford.

MEMORIALS
Hereford Cathedral; St Chad's Church, Shrewsbury.

BATTLE HONOURS
South Africa 1900–02.

'The Herefordshire Regiment in Gallipoli', showing the attack at Sulva Bay on 9th August 1915.

Soissonnais-Qurcq, Ypres 1918, Courtrai, France and Flanders 1918, Landing at Suvla, Rumani, Gaza, El Mughar, Jerusalem, Tell Asur.

Odon, Bourguebus Ridge, Souleuvre, Falaise, Antwerp, Hechtel, Venraij, Hochwald, Aller, North West Europe 1944–5.

LATER LINEAGE

Amalgamated in 1967 with the TA Battalions of other Light Infantry Regiments to form the Light Infantry Volunteers, with C Coy in Hereford. Redesignated as the 5th Battalion, The Light Infantry (Volunteers) in 1972. Redesignated as 5th (Shropshire and Herefordshire) Battalion, The Light Infantry (Volunteers) in 1988 and as 5th Battalion, The (Shropshire and Herefordshire) Light Infantry (Volunteers) in 1993. In 1999, the 5th Battalion, The (Shropshire and Herefordshire) Light Infantry (Volunters) was amalgamated with three other TA battalions in The West Midlands Regiment, which retains the Reconnaisance Platoon, E (Shropshire and Herefordshire Light Infantry) Company, in Hereford.

MUSEUMS

The Herefordshire Light Infantry Museum, TA Centre, Harold Street, Hereford HR1 2QX (telephone: 01432 359917) (by appointment only).

HERTFORDSHIRE

The Hertfordshire Regiment (TA)

ORIGINS AND DEVELOPMENT

Ten corps of rifle volunteers were raised in Hertfordshire in 1859–60 with a further four corps between 1867 and 1876. The original corps were formed into two administrative battalions covering the eastern and western parts of the county in October 1860. Consolidated in 1880, the two battalions became the 1st and 2nd (Hertfordshire) Volunteer Battalions, The Bedfordshire Regiment in 1887. In 1908 a single battalion was retained in the new Territorial Force as 1st Battalion, The Hertfordshire Regiment after pressure on the War Office to retain a clear county connection. Amalgamated 1961.

HISTORY

A service company went to South Africa to join the Bedfordshire Regiment in 1900. In the First World War, the 1/1st Battalion went to France in November 1914, spending four years on the Western Front. It participated in the battle of Loos on 15th September 1915, the latter stages of the battle of the Somme in 1916, and went over the top on the first day of the Third Battle of Ypres, popularly known as 'Passchendaele', on 31st July 1917 with 39th Division, taking heavy losses. It was again heavily engaged during the retreat in the face of the major German spring offensive in March 1918 around St Quentin. Subsequently, it played a major role in the forcing of the Hindenburg Line in September 1918, notably at Havrincourt. A second battalion was again formed in 1939 upon the doubling in size of the Territorial Army, the 1st Battalion being recruited in the east and the 2nd Battalion in the west of the county. The 1st Battalion served in home defence until going to Gibraltar in April 1943, but joined the 1st Infantry Division in Italy in July 1944,

A lifebelt from No. 9 Beach Group, used in the Normandy Landings in 1944, and now in Hertford Museum.

particularly distinguishing itself in the break-in of the German Gothic Line in September 1944. It transferred to Palestine in early 1945 before demobilisation in November 1946. The 2nd Battalion became the core battalion of No. 9 Beach Group in 1943, landing at La Rivière on Gold Beach on D-Day, 6th June 1944. In July 1944 it was retrained as infantry for front-line duties but, because of manpower shortages, it was disbanded in August 1944 and officers and men dispersed to other units. A single battalion was created upon reconstitution of the TA in 1947.

VICTORIA CROSSES
First World War (2). Of these, one is in the Regimental Museum and the other in that of the Bedfordshire and Hertfordshire Regiment at Luton.

BADGE
The Hart 'lodged' in water from the ancient badge of the county of Hertfordshire.

FACINGS
White.

REGIMENTAL MARCHES
'The Young May Moon'.

COLOURS
All Saints Church, Hertford.

MEMORIALS
All Saints Church, Hertford.

BATTLE HONOURS
South Africa, 1900–02.
Ypres 1914 '17, Festubert 1915, Loos, Somme 1916 '18, Ancre 1916, Pilckem, St Quentin, Rosieres, Lys, Hindenburg Line, Sambre, France and Flanders 1914–18.
Normandy Landing, North West Europe 1944, Montorsoli, Gothic Line, Monte Gamberaldi, Monte Ceco, Monte Grande, Italy 1944–45.

LATER LINEAGE
In 1961 The Hertfordshire Regiment (TA) was amalgamated with The Bedfordshire Regiment (TA) as The Bedfordshire and Hertfordshire Regiment (TA). In 1967 this was merged into the 5th (Volunteer) Battalion, The Royal Anglian Regiment. In 1996, the three volunteer battalions of The Royal Anglian Regiment were reduced to two with the Hertfordshire units becoming part of the 7th (Volunteer) Battalion. In 1999, the 7th (Volunteer) Battalion, The Royal Anglian Regiment was amalgamated with two other TA battalions as The East of England Regiment.

MUSEUMS
Hertford Museum, Bull Plain, Hertford SG14 1DT (telephone: 01992 582686; website: www.hertford.net/museum).

HUNTINGDONSHIRE
(see **The East Surrey Regiment**)

KENT

The Buffs (The Royal East Kent Regiment) (3rd Foot)

ORIGINS AND DEVELOPMENT

The 3rd Foot traces its origins to a company raised in 1572 by Captain Thomas Morgan from the London Trained Bands for the Dutch service. In 1665 its descendent regiment returned to the British establishment as the Holland Regiment, becoming in 1689 Prince George of Denmark's or the Lord High Admiral's Regiment. Known officially as The Buffs from 1751, it was affiliated to east Kent in 1782 and, in 1881, became The Buffs (the East Kent Regiment). A 2nd Battalion existed from 1857 to 1949. The Royal title was awarded by King George V in 1935. Amalgamated 1961.

HISTORY

Recruited in response to a plea for help from the Dutch in their war for independence against the Spanish, Morgan's company became the nucleus of four English regiments that served the Dutch until disbanded in 1665 with the outbreak of the Second Anglo-Dutch War. King Charles II then took the men into British service. The regiment took part in William III's defeat at Landen in July 1693, but then participated in all of Marlborough's victories. During the Peninsular War, the regiment's light company forced a passage of the Douro river on 12th May 1809, holding it until the regiment and the army could cross. At Albuhera on 16th May 1811 the regiment had 643 casualties out of 740 men engaged, losing and then regaining the Regimental Colour. Lieutenant Matthew Lathom managed to save the King's Colour from a French cavalryman, tearing the Colour from its staff and shoving it in his tunic. For his courage in defending the Colour, despite having his nose slashed off and his right arm severed, Lathom was presented with a gold medal by the officers of the regiment and later received surgery for his injuries at the personal expense of the Prince Regent. Lathom's medal is displayed at Canterbury and a magnificent silver mess centre-piece depicting the incident was commissioned for the regiment in 1872. Unfortunately, it wrongly shows Lathom as losing his left arm. An even more celebrated episode in the regiment's history occurred in the Third China War. Private John Moyse refused to kowtow to a Chinese Tartar mandarin, after capture on 13th August 1860, leading to his execution and immortality in Sir Francis Hastings Doyle's poem 'The Private of The Buffs'. In the First World War, the 6th, 7th and 8th Battalions all served and suffered heavily on the Somme in 1916, though the 8th Battalion went on to take a commanding feature on the Ypres-Commines Canal in June 1917, henceforth known as 'The Buffs Bank'. In the Second World War, the 1st Battalion suffered heavy losses at Alem Hamza in the Western Desert in December 1941 before being reformed as a motorised battalion, which fought at Alamein. Uniquely, the 7th Battalion was converted to armour and served in the North West Europe campaign of 1944–5.

VICTORIA CROSSES

Crimean War (2); Mohmand, 1897 (1); First World War (1). Of these, two are in the Regimental Museum.

NICKNAMES

The Old Buffs: from the buff-coloured jerkins and breeches of the London

Trained Bands still worn by those returning from the Netherlands in 1665.

The Buff Howards: to distinguish them from the Green Howards when both regiments were brigaded together and commanded by a Colonel Howard in the Fontenoy campaign.

The Nutcrackers: from the supposed prowess in cracking the heads of their enemies.

The Resurrectionists: from the speed of recovery on the field of Albuhera, though it is alternatively suggested that this name alludes to the antiquity of the regiment.

BADGE

The Green Dragon is assumed to be that of the Tudors, but it was not adopted as the regiment's badge until 1707, and not officially until 1751. Earlier, the badge had been a 'Sun in Splendour'.

MOTTOES

Veteri frondescit honore ('The glory of our fathers lives again in us').
Invicta ('Unconquered').

CUSTOMS

In deference to their London origins, The Buffs were permitted the privilege of marching through the City of London with drums beating, Colours flying and bayonets fixed from 1666 onwards. Every day, a former member of the regiment turns a page in the Book of Life (Remembrance) kept in the Warrior's Chapel in Canterbury Cathedral.

FACINGS

Buff. The regiment was permitted to retain buff on its drums and regimental Colour after becoming a Royal regiment.

REGIMENTAL MARCHES

'The Buffs' (quick march, supposedly composed by Handel).
'Men of Kent' (slow march).

COLOURS

Canterbury Cathedral.

MEMORIALS

The Chapel, Tower of London; Canterbury Cathedral; Kroonstad, South Africa.

BATTLE HONOURS

Blenheim, Ramillies, Oudenarde, Malplaquet, Dettingen, Guadaloupe 1759, Douro, Talavera, Albuhera, Vittoria, Pyrenees, Nivelle, Nive, Orthes, Toulouse, Peninsula, Punniar, Sevastopol, Taku Forts, South Africa 1879, Chitral, Relief of Kimberley, Paardeburg, South Africa 1900–02.

Aisne 1914, Ypres 1915 '17, Loos, Arras, Somme 1916 '18, Amiens, Hindenburg Line, Struma, Jerusalem, Baghdad.

North West Europe 1940, Alem Hamza, El Alamein, Robaa Valley, Sicily 1943, Trigno, Anzio, Argenta Gap, Leros, Shweli.

LATER LINEAGE

Amalgamated in 1961 with The Queen's Own Royal West Kent Regiment as The Queen's Own Buffs, The Royal Kent Regiment. In 1966 this, in turn, became the

The Buffs took part in the Third China War in 1860 and 'Taku Forts' is one of its battle honours. This is Beato's photograph of the British headquarters after the capture of the forts.

2nd Battalion of the new four-battalion The Queen's Regiment. Reduced to three battalions in 1973, The Queen's Regiment was amalgamated in 1992 with The Royal Hampshire Regiment as The Princess of Wales's Royal Regiment (Queen's and Royal Hampshires).

MUSEUMS

The Regimental Museum of The Buffs, Royal Museum and Art Gallery, High Street, Canterbury, Kent CT1 2RA (telephone: 01227 452747; fax: 01227 455047; website: www.canterbury.co.uk). Additional items are displayed at *The Princess of Wales's Royal Regiment and Queen's Regiment Museum*, Dover Castle, Dover, Kent CT16 1HU (telephone: 01227 818053; website: www.army.mod.uk/ceremonialandheritage/museums).

The Queen's Own Royal West Kent Regiment
(50th and 97th Foot)

ORIGINS AND DEVELOPMENT

The 50th was raised in 1756 and affiliated to west Kent in 1782. It received its royal title in 1831 as The Queen's Own Regiment. The 97th was raised by the Earl of Ulster in 1824. They were linked in 1881 as the 1st and 2nd Battalions, The Queen's Own Royal West Kent Regiment. Reduced to a single battalion in 1948. Amalgamated 1961.

HISTORY

The 50th was originally numbered the 52nd Foot but was renumbered after eleven months when the 50th and 51st regiments were both disbanded following their surrender to the French at Oswego in North America. The regiment's first active service was the abortive expedition to seize the French coastal fortress at Rochefort in September 1757. The 50th then served in Germany and Ireland before being briefly embarked as marines in 1778. Serving at Gibraltar when the French Revolutionary Wars began, the 50th took part in amphibious operations against Corsica in 1794 and in the expedition to Egypt in 1801. A stint in Copenhagen in 1807 was followed by service in the Peninsula, where the 50th won eight battle honours. Associated from 1827 with the Duke of Clarence, the regiment was styled The Queen's Own by his order after he had become King William IV in 1831. The Crimea was the active debut of the 97th, which went on to the Indian Mutiny while the 50th went to New Zealand. During the First World War the regiment raised eighteen battalions. The 1st Battalion distinguished itself in taking Hill 60 near Ypres on 17th April 1915. The 8th Battalion took heavy casualties at Loos in September 1915, while a few men of the 1st Battalion reached the German lines at High Wood on 22nd July 1916. Battalions also fought in Gallipoli, Mesopotamia, Palestine and Italy. In June 1940, the 1st, 4th and 5th Battalions served together in a 'Queen's Own Brigade' during the retreat to Dunkirk. In addition the 6th and 7th Battalions suffered very heavy casualties. The 2nd Battalion was in Malta and in the doomed Dodecanese campaign, most servicemen being captured on Leros in September 1943. The 4th and 5th Battalions took part in the battle of El Alamein, whilst the 1st and 6th Battalions landed in North Africa. Later the 1st Battalion served in Italy and then in Greece, and the 5th and 6th Battalions saw the fighting in Italy to the end. In April 1944 the 4th Battalion garrisoned Kohima in Assam with about 260 of the Assam Regiment, a focus for the major Japanese offensive intended as a 'march on Delhi'. For sixteen days, the heavily outnumbered regiment held Garrison Hill in often hand-to-hand fighting against a full Japanese division until relieved by the 1st Battalion, The Royal Berkshire Regiment on 21st April. The 'Kohima Cross', originally carved by Robert Clinch in 1944 and bearing the names of those who fell in the epic defence, stands at the museum entrance in Canterbury. Post-war service included a tour of Malaya during the Emergency, and then the Suez Canal operation in 1956, followed by a full tour during the Cyprus Emergency.

VICTORIA CROSSES

Crimean War (2); First World War (3); Second World War (1). Of these, four are in the Regimental Museum.

NICKNAMES

The Dirty Half Hundred (50th): from the original black facings.

The Celestials (97th): from the original sky-blue facings derived from the ribbon of the Order of St Patrick associated with the Earl of Ulster.

The Blind Half Hundred: given to the 50th during the Egyptian Campaign of 1801 because many men suffered from ophthalmia, which caused temporary or sometimes permanent loss of sight.

BADGE

The White Horse was the ancient badge of Kent, supposedly ascribed to the Saxon brothers Horsa and Hencgest (Hengist) who established the kingdom of Kent in the fifth century AD.

MOTTO
Quo fas et gloria ducunt ('Where right and glory lead').
Invicta ('Unconquered').

FACINGS
Royal blue.

REGIMENTAL MARCHES
'A Hundred Pipers' (quick march).
'Men of Kent' (slow march).

COLOURS
All Saints Church, Maidstone.

MEMORIALS
Brenchly Gardens, Maidstone; All Saints Church, Maidstone.

BATTLE HONOURS
Vimiera, Corunna, Almarez, Vittoria, Pyrenees, Nive, Orthes, Peninsula, Punniar, Moodkee, Ferozeshah, Aliwal, Sobraon, Alma, Inkerman, Sevastopol, Lucknow, New Zealand, Egypt 1882, Nile 1884–85, South Africa 1900–02, Afghanistan 1919.

Mons, Ypres 1914 '15 '17 '18, Hill 60, Somme 1916 '18, Vimy 1917, Italy 1917–18, Gallipoli 1915, Gaza, Defence of Kut al Amara, Shargat.

North West Europe 1940, El Alamein, Medjez Plain, Centuripe, Sangro, Cassino, Trasimene Line, Argenta Gap, Malta 1940–2, Defence of Kohima.

LATER LINEAGE
Amalgamated in 1961 with The Buffs (The Royal East Kent Regiment) as The Queen's Own Buffs, The Royal Kent Regiment. In 1966 this, in turn, became the 2nd Battalion of the new four-battalion The Queen's Regiment. Reduced to three battalions in 1973, The Queen's Regiment was amalgamated in 1992 with The Royal Hampshire Regiment as The Princess of Wales's Royal Regiment (Queen's and Royal Hampshires).

MUSEUMS
The Queen's Own Royal West Kent Regiment Museum, Maidstone Museum and Bentlif Art Gallery, St Faith's Street, Maidstone, Kent ME14 1LH (telephone: 01622 754497). Additional items are displayed in *The Princess of Wales's Royal Regiment and Queen's Regiment Museum*, Dover Castle, Dover, Kent CT16 1HU (telephone: 01227 818053; website: www.army.mod.uk/ceremonialandheritage/museums).

LANCASHIRE

The East Lancashire Regiment
(30th and 59th Foot)

ORIGINS AND DEVELOPMENT

The original 30th was raised in 1689 as Castleton's Regiment, only to be disbanded in 1695 and then reformed in 1702 as Saunderson's Marines. The 59th was raised in 1755. In 1782 the 30th was affiliated to Cambridgeshire and the 59th to Nottinghamshire. Linked in 1881 as the 1st and 2nd Battalions, The East Lancashire Regiment. Reduced to a single battalion in 1948. Amalgamated 1958.

HISTORY

As marines the 30th served at Gibraltar and aboard at several naval engagements in the Mediterranean. It suffered another disbandment in 1713, only to be restored once more two years later. The regiment served as marines again from 1745 to 1748, participating in the naval battle off Cape Finisterre and in the Seven Years War, raiding the French coast at Belleisle in 1761. Both the 30th and the 59th served in the American War of Independence. In the French Revolutionary War the 30th was afloat once more before taking part in the victory over the French army at Alexandria in 1801. It became the first British regiment to garrison Malta. At Salamanca on 22nd July 1812 Ensign John Pratt of the 30th captured the eagle of the French 22nd Regiment. Presented to the Prince Regent and lodged in the Royal Hospital, Chelsea, it was returned to the regiment in 1947. At Waterloo on 18th June 1815, the 30th also captured the drum of the French 105th Regiment. The 59th, meanwhile, took part in the seizure of the Cape of Good Hope from the Dutch in 1806. The 59th again showed great gallantry in the assault on the Jat stronghold of Bhurtpore on 18th January 1826 and won the unique battle honour of Canton for its participation in the capture of the Chinese city by an international force on 29th

The 2nd Battalion 30th Foot storms the walls of Badajoz during the Peninsular War.

57

Drummer Spencer John Bent of the 1st Battalion, The East Lancashire Regiment, winning his VC at Le Gheer, November 1914, rescuing a wounded man under fire.

December 1857. Treasures of the 59th include the 'Seahorse Silver' rescued from the wreck of the troopship *Seahorse* in 1816, which includes a silver snuff box and two silver forks, and the 'Canton Bell' acquired from a Chinese temple in 1857. On 1st July 1916 on the Somme, the 11th Battalion (The Accrington Pals) suffered 584 casualties from the 720 men who went over the top at Serre. In 1944 the 1st Battalion liberated the Dutch city of 'sHertogenbosch in five days of almost continuous action, fighting in cold and wet weather with few supplies and suffering 25 per cent casualties.

VICTORIA CROSSES
    Crimean War (1); Second Afghan War (1); First World War (4); Second World War (1). Of these, two are displayed in the Regimental Museum in Blackburn, one in the Museum of Lancashire, and one in Towneley Hall.

NICKNAMES
    The Three Tens (30th): from the Roman numerals XXX (30).
    The Yellow Bellies: from the 30th's original primrose-yellow facings.
    The Lily Whites: from the 59th's original white facings.

BADGE
    The Red Rose is that of Lancashire, while the Sphinx and 'Egypt' was awarded for service at Alexandria in 1801. The laurel wreath was awarded to the 30th for its role at Waterloo on 18th June 1815, where it was positioned near the centre of the allied line.

MOTTO
    Spectemur agendo ('Let us be judged by our deeds').

CUSTOMS
1st July became the Regimental Day following the service and losses suffered by both the 1st and 11th Battalions on the Somme. The 59th celebrated Ahmed Khel Day (19th April) for this action in 1880 during the Second Afghan War, in which Captain E. H. Sartorius won the Victoria Cross.

FACINGS
White.

REGIMENTAL MARCHES
'L'Attaque' (Quick march, originally that of the 30th).
'God Bless the Prince of Wales' (slow march).
'The Lancashire Lad' (59th).

COLOURS
Blackburn Cathedral; Ely Cathedral (30th).

MEMORIALS
Garrison Church of St Alban, Fulwood; Blackburn Cathedral; Waterloo; Tramore Bay, Ireland (59th lost on *Seahorse*); Old Colonial Cemetery, Hong Kong (59th); Kukrail, Lucknow, India (30th); Burnley Parish Church (South African War); Nottingham Castle (59th, Second Afghan War); Luke Copse, Serre, Somme (Accrington Pals); Braamfontein, Johannesburg, South Africa (1st Battalion).

BATTLE HONOURS
Gibraltar 1704–5, Cape of Good Hope 1806, Corunna, Java, Badajoz, Salamanca, Vittoria, St Sebastian, Nive, Peninsula, Waterloo, Bhurtpore, Alma, Inkerman, Sevastopol, Canton, Ahmed Khel, Afghanistan 1878–9, Chitral, South Africa 1900–02.
Retreat from Mons, Marne 1914, Aisne 1914 '18, Ypres 1914 '15 '18, Neuve Chapelle, Arras 1917–18, Somme 1916–18, Helles, Doiran 1917–18, Kut al Amara.
Dunkirk 1940, Falaise, Lower Maas, Ourthe, Reichswald, Weeze, Aller, Madagascar, Pinwe, Burma 1944–5.

LATER LINEAGE
Amalgamated in 1958 with The South Lancashire Regiment (The Prince of Wales's Volunteers) as The Lancashire Regiment. In 1970 The Lancashire Regiment was amalgamated with The Loyal Regiment (North Lancashire) as The Queen's Lancashire Regiment.

MUSEUMS
Blackburn Museum and Art Gallery, Museum Street, Blackburn, Lancashire BB1 7AJ (telephone: 01254 667130; website: www.army.mod.uk /ceremonialandheritage/museums). Additional items are to be found in *Towneley Hall*, Burnley, Lancashire BB11 3RQ (telephone: 01282 424213; fax: 01282 436138); *The Museum of Lancashire*, Old Sessions House, Stanley Street, Preston, Lancashire PR2 9WL (telephone: 01772 264075); and *Museum of The Queen's Lancashire Regiment*, Fulwood Barracks, Preston, Lancashire PR2 8AA (telephone: 01772 260362; fax: 01772 260583).

The King's Own Royal Regiment (Lancaster)
(4th Foot)

ORIGINS AND DEVELOPMENT

The 4th Foot was raised as the 2nd Tangier Regiment in 1680, becoming the Duchess of York and Albany's Regiment four years later. With the accession of the Duke of York as King James II in 1685, it became The Queen's Regiment and, in 1715, The King's Own. It was not given a specific territorial designation until 1881, as The King's Own (Royal Lancaster Regiment). A 2nd Battalion existed from 1857 to 1949. Amalgamated 1959.

HISTORY

Though raised for service at Tangier, the regiment saw no actual combat there, returning to England in 1684. It fought at Sedgemoor against the Duke of Monmouth's rebel army on 16th June 1685 and then served in Ireland. It spent the remainder of the Nine Years War in Flanders and was on the marine establishment for much of the War of Spanish Succession, participating in the capture of Gibraltar in August 1704. At Culloden on 16th April 1746 the 4th bore the brunt of the charge of the Highlanders of the Jacobite army. The regiment fought in the first engagements of the American War of Independence at Lexington and Bunker Hill on 19th April and 17th June 1775. At Badajoz on 6th April 1812, Private Hatton captured the Colour of the German Hesse Darmstadt Regiment in the service of the

Private Harry Christian, of the 2nd Battalion, The King's Own (Royal Lancaster Regiment), receives his Victoria Cross from King George V in Glasgow in September 1917. Christian won the VC for digging out, under fire, three comrades buried by a shell at Givenchy on 18th October 1915. His VC is on display in the regimental museum.

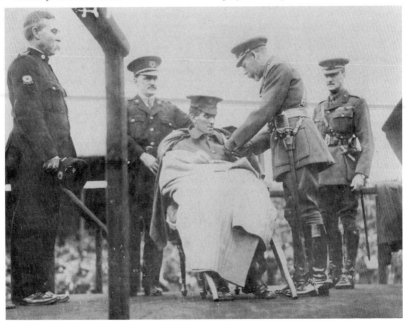

French. The silver medal presented to Private Hatton by his comrades after his exploits at Badajoz remains in the regiment's possession, though the Colour of the Hesse Darmstadt Regiment that he took is in the Great Hall of the Royal Hospital, Chelsea. After service in the Anglo-American War of 1812–14, the 4th again distinguished itself at Waterloo on 18th June 1815. During the Crimean War the regiment was present at the Alma and Inkerman before being sent to assist in the suppression of the latter stages of the Indian Mutiny. The 1/4th Battalion saw further service in Abyssinia in 1867–8 and the 2/4th in Zululand in 1879. The 2nd Battalion was one of three Lancashire battalions caught by the deadly fire of the Boers on the summit of Spion Kop (Spioenkop) on 24th January 1900 in one of the attempts to break through to relieve the British garrison trapped in Ladysmith. Eight Victoria Crosses were won in the First World War, in which the 1st Battalion was badly mauled at Le Cateau on 26th August 1914 and the 2nd at Frezenburg on 8th May 1915. The 6th Battalion served throughout the Dardanelles campaign while the 8th managed to impose a significant delay on the German advance on 21st March 1918. The 11th was one of the 'Bantam' battalions of fit but undersized men, in this case mostly recruited from Lancashire and Cumbrian miners. In the Second World War the 1st Battalion took heavy losses on Leros in December 1943. Reformed with reinforcements from the 8th Battalion, it subsequently won the unique battle honour of Montone in June 1944 during the Italian campaign.

VICTORIA CROSSES
Crimean War (1); First World War (8). Of these, five are in the Regimental Museum.

NICKNAMES
Barrell's Blues: from Colonel William Barrell, who commanded 1734–49, and the Royal title granted in 1715.
The Lions: from the badge.

BADGE
The Royal Lion of England is said to have been granted by King William III, traditionally because of the regiment's early switch in allegiance to him in 1688.

MOTTO
Honi soit qui mal y pense ('Let him who thinks evil of it be ashamed').

CUSTOMS
The regiment traditionally celebrated St George's Day (23rd April) from at least 1704 through its royal connections. From 1908 onwards, all ranks wore a red rose in the head-dress, a wreath of red roses was placed on the Colours, and the drums were garlanded. On dinner nights in the officers' mess, the silver beaker carried by Lieutenant Francis Maguire, who was killed leading the forlorn hope in an assault on the fortress of San Sebastian on 31st August 1813, was placed in front of the commanding officer. Earlier, Maguire had taken a French Colour at Salamanca on 22nd July 1812.

FACINGS
Royal blue.

REGIMENTAL MARCHES
'Corn Riggs are Bonnie' (quick march).

'Trelawny' (slow march).

COLOURS

Priory Church, Lancaster; Scottish United Services Museum, Edinburgh Castle (those carried at Culloden); Hartburn Parish Church; King's Chapel, Gibraltar; Ulverston Parish Church (4th Battalion).

MEMORIALS

Priory Church, Lancaster; Spion Kop (Spioenkop) and Wynne Hill, Tugela Heights, KwaZulu-Natal, South Africa (2nd Battalion).

BATTLE HONOURS

Namur 1695, Gibraltar 1704–5, Guadaloupe 1759, St Lucia 1778, Corunna, Badajoz, Salamanca, Vittoria, St Sebastian, Nive, Peninsula, Bladensburg, Waterloo, Alma, Inkerman, Sevastopol, Abyssinia, South Africa 1879, Relief of Ladysmith, South Africa 1900–02.

Marne 1914, Ypres 1915 '17, Somme 1916 '18, Arras 1917 '18, Messines 1917, Lys, France and Flanders 1914–18, Macedonia 1915–18, Gallipoli 1915, Mesopotamia 1916–18.

Dunkirk 1940, North West Europe 1940, Defence of Habbaniya, Merjayun, Tobruk Sortie, North Africa 1940–2, Montone, Lamone Bridgehead, Malta 1941–2, Chindits 1944.

LATER LINEAGE

Amalgamated in 1959 with The Border Regiment as The King's Own Royal Border Regiment.

MUSEUMS

King's Own Royal Regiment Museum, Market Square, Lancaster LA1 1HT (telephone: 01524 64637; fax: 01524 841692; e-mail: kingsownmuseum@iname.com).

A mortar platoon, 1st Battalion, The King's Own Royal Border Regiment in Jordan, photographed by Peter Donnelly.

The King's Regiment (Liverpool)
(8th Foot)

ORIGINS AND DEVELOPMENT

The 8th Foot was raised in Derbyshire, Hertfordshire and London in June 1685 as Princess Anne of Denmark's Regiment, the title changing to The Queen's when Anne succeeded to the throne in 1702. On Anne's death, it became The King's. In 1881 the regiment received the title of The King's (Liverpool Regiment), subsequently amended to The King's Regiment (Liverpool) in 1921. A 2nd Battalion existed from 1857 to 1948 and regular 3rd and 4th Battalions between 1900 and 1906. Amalgamated 1959.

HISTORY

The new regiment became embroiled in controversy when Lieutenant Colonel Beaumont and five of its officers – the 'Portsmouth Captains' – were court-martialled for refusing to enlist Irish recruits at Portsmouth. Within a few months, William III had landed in England and Beaumont was reinstated. The regiment's first action was at the Boyne in July 1690. In 1702 it took part in the capture of Venlo in the Netherlands, took over one thousand French prisoners at Blenheim on 13th August 1704 and spearheaded Marlborough's attack at Malplaquet on 11th September 1709. Between 1815 and 1860, the 8th spent thirty-eight years overseas, a fourteen-year tour of India beginning in 1846. During the Indian Mutiny, the regiment took part in the assault and subsequent five days of hand-to-hand fighting for control of Delhi in September 1857. Immediately after the fall of Delhi, the 8th was sent to relieve Agra, covering 54 miles (87 km) in thirty-six hours and helping to defeat a rebel force of seven thousand men on arrival. The 2/8th spent its early years in Ireland and the Mediterranean before going to India in 1877. At Peiwar Kotal on 2nd December 1878 it was part of the force making a feint attack while Sir Frederick (later Lord) Roberts outflanked the Afghan position in this early engagement of the Second Afghan War. In the First World War, the 8th and 10th Battalions respectively were the Liverpool Irish and the Liverpool Scottish. The medical officer of the latter was Captain Noel Chavasse of the Royal Army Medical Corps, who won the Victoria Cross with the battalion at Guillemont on 9th August 1916; he was subsequently awarded a posthumous bar to his Victoria Cross in 1917. In the Second World War, the 13th Battalion was part of Wingate's first Chindit operation behind Japanese lines in Burma in February 1943, while the 1st Battalion took part in the second Chindit operation in March 1944. After service in Italy, and following the German withdrawal from Greece and the outbreak of civil war between nationalist and communist factions, the 2nd Battalion helped restore the authority of the Greek National Government in Athens in December 1944.

VICTORIA CROSSES

South African War (3); First World War (6). Of these, seven are in the Regimental Museum.

NICKNAMES

The Leather Hats: supposedly from an incident in the American War of Independence, when those who had lost their own head-dress replaced it with the leather head-dress of their opponents.

BADGE
The White Horse of Hanover was originally borne by the grenadier companies of all battalions following the accession of King George I in 1715. The motto below was also borne by all regiments that had the White Horse as a badge, being that of the Royal Hanoverian Guelphic Order.

MOTTO
Nec aspera terrent (Nor do difficulties deter).

FACINGS
Royal blue.

REGIMENTAL MARCHES
'Here's to the Maiden'.
'Zachmi Dill'.
'The English Rose'.

COLOURS
Anglican Cathedral, Liverpool; Salisbury Cathedral.

MEMORIALS
William Brown Street, Liverpool (nineteenth-century campaigns); Whitley Gardens, Shaw Street, Liverpool (Indian Mutiny); Tunnel Hill, Ladysmith, KwaZulu-Natal, South Africa (1st Battalion); Lydenburg, South Africa (1st Battalion).

BATTLE HONOURS
Blenheim, Ramillies, Oudenarde, Malplaquet, Dettingen, Martinique 1809, Niagara, Delhi 1857, Lucknow, Peiwar Kotal, Afghanistan 1878–80, Burma 1885–7, Defence of Ladysmith, South Africa 1899–1902, Afghanistan 1919.
Retreat from Mons, Marne 1914, Aisne 1914, Ypres 1914 '15 '17, Festubert 1915, Loos, Somme 1916 '18, Arras 1917 '18, Scarpe 1917 '18, Cambrai 1917 '18.
Normandy Landing, Cassino II, Trasimene Line, Tuori, Capture of Forli, Rimini Line, Athens, Chindits 1943 '44.

LATER LINEAGE
Amalgamated in 1959 with The Manchester Regiment as The King's Regiment (Manchester and Liverpool). In 1969 it became The King's Regiment.

MUSEUMS
City Soldiers, The King's Regiment Collection, *Museum of Liverpool Life*, Pier Head, Liverpool L3 1PZ (telephone: 0151 478 4080; website: www.nmgm.org.uk/liverpoollife).

The Lancashire Fusiliers
(20th Foot)

ORIGINS AND DEVELOPMENT
The 20th was raised in 1688 as Peyton's Regiment. In 1782 it was affiliated to east Devonshire but, in 1881, became the Lancashire Fusiliers. A 2nd Battalion existed from 1858 to 1948 and from 1952 to 1954, while 3rd and 4th Battalions existed

between 1898 and 1906. The 20th Foot became the 4th Battalion, The Royal Regiment of Fusiliers in 1968.

HISTORY

One of the new regiments raised after William III's landing in England, the 20th saw its first service in Ireland, where it remained until 1702. One of six regiments then selected for marine service, it formed part of the expedition to Cadiz. It was in Portugal from 1707 to 1712 and helped defend Gibraltar against the Spanish in 1727. It was at Dettingen, Fontenoy and Culloden, coming under the command of James Wolfe in 1750, the regiment's collections including Wolfe's sword, sash, ring and ruffles. Subsequently, while Wolfe went to North America, the regiment served in the Duke of Brunswick's allied army in Germany, being one of the six regiments to win enduring fame at Minden on 1st August 1759. In the American War of Independence, the 20th was one of those regiments compelled to surrender at Saratoga in 1777, the Colours being burned so that they could not fall into American hands. The French Revolutionary War saw the regiment initially serving in the West Indies. Both the 1/20th and the newly raised 2/20th served at Egmont-op-Zee in 1799 and in Egypt in 1801. One celebrated member of the regiment was Major-General Robert Ross, who commanded the victorious British force at Bladensburg in 1814, leading to the capture of Washington during the Anglo-American War (1812–14), only to be killed in a skirmish at Baltimore. The 2nd Battalion, raised once more in 1858, provided the first British troops sent to Japan in 1864 following the murder of a number of Europeans. Subsequently, the 2nd Battalion served in the reconquest of the Sudan, one of its casualties to disease being Major 'Roddy' Owen, a famed sportsman who had won the Grand National in 1892. At Spion Kop on 24th January 1900 the 2nd Battalion, together with the 2nd King's Own Royal Regiment (Lancaster) and the 1st South Lancashire Regiment (The Prince of Wales's Volunteers), was exposed to murderous fire from the Boers, an action defined by the publication of photographs that shocked the Victorian public by showing heaps of British dead awaiting burial in a trench. On 25th April 1915 the 1st Battalion won six Victoria Crosses 'before breakfast', landing on W Beach (Lancashire Landing) at Cape Helles on Gallipoli from small open boats at the cost of 361 casualties. A reminder of Cape Helles is the ship's bell of HMS *Euryalus*, from which the regiment's boats were launched. In the Second World War the 1st Battalion was part of the second Chindit expedition in March 1944, while the 2nd Battalion served in Tunisia, Sicily and Italy and the 10th Battalion fought against the Japanese in trying conditions in the Arakan from October 1942 to May 1943.

VICTORIA CROSSES

First World War (17); Second World War (1). Of these, five are in the Regimental Museum.

NICKNAMES

The Minden Boys: from the battle of Minden.
Two Tens: from the regimental number.

BADGE

The Sphinx in a laurel wreath and 'Egypt' within a grenade reflects both service in Egypt in 1801 and the status of Fusiliers, the grenade being borne to commemorate the original role of fusiliers in protecting artillery. Why the 20th became designated as Fusiliers in 1881 is unclear.

MOTTOES
Omnia audax ('Daring in all things').
Honi soit qui mal y pense ('Let him who thinks evil of it be ashamed').

CUSTOMS
While leading ceremonial parades, the regiment maintained the tradition of pioneers wearing buck-skin aprons and gauntlets and carrying axes. As with other Minden regiments, the anniversary was marked by red and yellow roses being worn in head-dresses and decoration of the drums. In addition, any officer who had not previously done so would eat a rose from a silver finger bowl filled with champagne. Gallipoli Sunday was also observed in Bury on the Sunday nearest to 25th April, the annual event since becoming one to commemorate all Lancashire Fusiliers who have fallen in the service of their country.

FACINGS
White.

REGIMENTAL MARCHES
'The British Grenadiers'.
'The Minden March'.

COLOURS
St Mary's Church, Bury.

MEMORIALS
St Mary's Church, Bury; Wellington Barracks, Bury (First and Second World Wars); Whitehead Gardens, Bury (South African War); Salford (First World War Territorial and New Army Battalions); Rochdale Parish Church (2/6th Battalion, First World War) and Memorial Gardens (Second World War); Exeter Cathedral (20th, Crimean War); Lancashire Landing Cemetery, Cape Helles, Gallipoli, Turkey (1st Battalion); Spion Kop (Spioenkop), KwaZulu-Natal, South Africa (2nd Battalion).

BATTLE HONOURS
Dettingen, Minden, Egmont-op-Zee, Maida, Vimiero, Corunna, Vittoria, Pyrenees, Orthes, Toulouse, Peninsula, Alma, Inkerman, Sevastopol, Lucknow, Khartoum, Relief of Ladysmith, South Africa 1900–02.
Retreat from Mons, Aisne 1914 '18, Ypres 1915 '17 '18, Somme 1916 '18, Arras 1917 '18, Passchendaele, Cambrai 1917 '18, Hindenburg Line, Macedonia 1915–18, Landing at Helles.
Defence of Escaut, Caen, Medjez el Bab, Sangro, Cassino II, Argenta Gap, Malta 1941–2, Kohima, Chindits 1944, Burma 1943–5.

LATER LINEAGE
4th Battalion, The Royal Regiment of Fusiliers was disbanded in 1969.

MUSEUMS
The Fusiliers Museum Lancashire, Wellington Barracks, Bolton Road, Bury, Lancashire BL8 2PL (telephone: 0161 764 2208; website: www.army.mod.uk /ceremonialandheritage/museums).

The Loyal Regiment (North Lancashire)
(47th and 81st Foot)

ORIGINS AND DEVELOPMENT

The 47th was raised in Scotland in 1741 as Mordaunt's Regiment, becoming affiliated to Lancashire in 1782. The 81st was raised as the Loyal Lincoln Volunteers from the Lincolnshire Militia in 1793, the title being awarded as the militia had volunteered *en masse*. They were linked as the 1st and 2nd Battalions, The Loyal North Lancashire Regiment in 1881. In 1921 the title was changed to the Loyal Regiment (North Lancashire). Reduced to a single battalion in 1949. Amalgamated 1970.

HISTORY

The 47th's first action was against the Jacobites of the Young Pretender at Prestonpans in 1745. Five years later it sailed for Canada and took part in the capture of Louisburg. Occupying a central position in the British line on the Heights of Abraham before Quebec in 1759, the regiment became known as 'Wolfe's Own'. It was at Bunker Hill in 1775 and was part of the army under John Burgoyne forced to surrender to the Americans at Saratoga on 17th October 1777. The 2/47th took part in the Peninsular War, particularly distinguishing itself at Tarifa on 31st December 1812. The 81st served in the West Indies and at the Cape of Good Hope before arriving back in the Mediterranean and taking part in the victory at Maida in southern Italy on 4th July 1806. Following Maida, Colonel (later General Sir) James Kempt, commanding the 81st, dined on a tortoise. Later, he had the shell of the 'Maida Tortoise' mounted in silver as a snuff box for the officers' mess. Six Russian drums were captured by the 47th at Inkerman on 5th November 1854. In the South African War, the 1st Battalion earned the unique battle honour of 'Defence of Kimberley', four companies having been sent there at the outbreak of the war to defend the diamond mines. The battalion's commanding officer, Lieutenant Colonel R. G. Kekewich, conducted the defence, more often than not hampered by the

This official photograph postcard from the First World War is captioned 'Men of the Loyal North Lancashire Regiment cheering gaily when ordered to take turn in the trenches'.

B Company, 1st Battalion, The Loyal Regiment (North Lancashire) waiting on an improvised runway to be airlifted to the Malay/Thai border in 1959.

mining magnate Cecil Rhodes. Two fine silver centre-pieces in the possession of The Queen's Lancashire Regiment are replicas of the memorial to the regiment in Kimberley, presented to the officers' and sergeants' messes by the citizens of Kimberley and Beaconsfield in South Africa in 1908. In the First World War, the 2nd Battalion took part in operations in German East Africa, hence another unique battle honour, 'Kilimanjaro'. In the Second World War, the 2nd and 5th Battalions (the latter having converted to the 18th Regiment, Reconnaissance Corps) were captured by the Japanese at the fall of Singapore on 15th February 1942. After the war, the 1st Battalion had a tour in Malaya during the latter stages of the Malayan Emergency.

VICTORIA CROSSES
Crimean War (1); First World War (3); Second World War (1). None are in the Regimental Museum.

NICKNAMES
Wolfe's Own (47th): from service at Quebec.
The Cauliflowers (47th): from the regimental rose badge.

BADGE
The Royal Crest and the Red Rose of Lancaster.

MOTTO
Loyauté m'oblige ('Loyalty binds me').

CUSTOMS
To commemorate Major-General James Wolfe, the 47th traditionally wore a black line in the officer's gold lace, though in reality the line had been adopted as early as 1751. The collar badge was that of the Arms of the City of Lincoln, a fleur-de-lis on a Cross of St George.

FACINGS
   White.

REGIMENTAL MARCHES
   'The Red Red Rose' (quick march).
   'The 47th Regimental Slow March' (slow march).
   'The Mountain Rose' (47th).
   'The Lincolnshire Poacher' (81st).

COLOURS
   St John's Church, Preston; Museum of Lancashire, Preston.

MEMORIALS
   St John's Church, Preston; Avenham Park, Preston (South African War); Queen's Park, Bolton (First World War); Corfe Castle Church, Dorset; Cerny-en-Laonnais, Soissons, France (Aisne, 1914); North Gate Cemetery, Baghdad (6th Battalion).

BATTLE HONOURS
   Louisburg, Quebec 1759, Maida, Corunna, Tarifa, Vittoria, St Sebastian, Nive, Peninsula, Ava, Alma, Inkerman, Sevastopol, Ali Masjid, Afghanistan 1878–9, Defence of Kimberley, South Africa 1899–1902.
   Mons, Aisne 1914 '18, Ypres 1914 '17 '18, Somme 1916 '18, Lys, Hindenburg Line, Gaza, Baghdad, Sulva, Kilimanjaro.
   Dunkirk 1940, Djebel Kesskiss, Gueriat el Aatch Ridge, Africa 1943, Anzio, Fiesole, Monte Grande, Italy 1944–5, Jahore, Singapore Island.

LATER LINEAGE
   Amalgamated in 1970 with The Lancashire Regiment (Prince of Wales's Volunteers) as The Queen's Lancashire Regiment.

MUSEUMS
   Museum of The Queen's Lancashire Regiment, Fulwood Barracks, Preston, Lancashire PR2 8AA (telephone: 01772 260362; fax: 01772 260583). Additional items are displayed in *The Museum of Lancashire*, Old Sessions House, Stanley Street, Preston, Lancashire PR2 9WL (telephone: 01772 260362).

The South Lancashire Regiment (The Prince of Wales's Volunteers) (40th and 82nd Foot)

ORIGINS AND DEVELOPMENT
   The 40th was raised in Nova Scotia in 1717 as Philip's Regiment and affiliated to Somerset in 1782, while the 82nd was raised in Stamford in 1793 as The Prince of Wales's Volunteers. In 1881 the two were linked as The South Lancashire Regiment (The Prince of Wales's Volunteers). Between 1923 and 1938 the regiment was known as The Prince of Wales's Volunteers (South Lancashire). Reduced to a single battalion in 1948. Amalgamated 1958.

HISTORY
   Raised from independent companies in Nova Scotia, the 40th remained in Canada for its first forty-four years, seeing service at the capture of Louisburg in 1758 and

The Germantown Medal.

Quebec in 1759. After further service in the West Indies, the 40th arrived in Britain for the first time in 1765. Recalled to North America during the American War of Independence, the regiment was present at the battles of Brooklyn, Princeton, Brandywine and Germantown. To commemorate the fighting withdrawal of the 40th, which was in support of the British outposts when the Americans attacked at Germantown on 4th October 1777, Lieutenant Colonel Musgrave had the unique Germantown Medal struck, the first authenticated British award for field service and the forerunner of the campaign medal. In the French Revolutionary and Napoleonic Wars, the 40th was one of the regiments in support of an abortive landing by a French émigré force at Quiberon Bay in 1793 and, later, the 1/40th took part in the disastrous expedition to Monte Video in 1807. In the First Afghan War (1839–42) the 40th was heavily engaged in the initial successful advance towards Kabul and Kandahar, its subsequent battle honours reflecting the contemporary English spelling of Cabool and Candahar. The 40th was also in action against the Marathas at Maharajpore in the Gwalior campaign on 29th December 1843 and, on 3rd December 1854, stormed the Eureka Stockade held by disgruntled Australian gold miners. The Maharajpore drum was captured from the Marathas in December 1843 and, though damaged in a fire in 1891, the shell was preserved. The 82nd, meanwhile, secured the 'Sevastopol Bell' at the fall of the Russian Crimean fortress on 10th September 1855 and the 'Rajah's Bed-post', actually a ceremonial staff of beaten silver later carried by the regiment's drum-major, at Lucknow on 14th November 1857. During the South African War, the 1st Battalion was one of those Lancashire regiments that suffered heavy casualties at Spion Kop on 24th January 1900 in an attempt to relieve the British garrison at Ladysmith. In the First World War the South Lancs was represented not only on the Western Front but also in Macedonia and Mesopotamia. In the Second World War the 2nd Battalion led the crossing of the Irrawaddy at the Nyaungu Bridgehead in the advance to Rangoon in Burma.

VICTORIA CROSSES
Second Maori War (1); First World War (4). Of these, two are in the Regimental Museum.

NICKNAMES
The Fighting Fortieth: from the regimental number.
The Excellers: from the Roman numerals XL (40).

BADGE
As with the East Lancashire Regiment, the Sphinx and 'Egypt' were awarded for service in Egypt in 1801 (by the 40th) and the laurel wreath for Waterloo (again the 40th). The Prince of Wales's Plume is that of the 82nd, while the motto is also that of the Prince of Wales.

MOTTO
Ich Dien ('I serve').

CUSTOMS
The 40th wore a black stripe in their lace in memory of James Wolfe's death at

Quebec in 1759 and subsequently continued to do so in additional memory of General Sir James Abercombie, killed at the moment of victory at Alexandria in 1801. A silver statuette, modelled on 2nd Lieutenant S. W. 'Sam' Boast of the 2nd Battalion and sculpted in 1930 as a memorial to those officers who served during the First World War, was never polished in order to represent the feel of the mud of Flanders, but the helmet was always shiny from the many officers who customarily touched it as a mark of respect.

FACINGS
White.

REGIMENTAL MARCHES
'God Bless the Prince of Wales' (quick march, originally of the 82nd).
'Lancashire Witches' (slow march).
'The Somerset Poacher' (40th).

COLOURS
St Elphin's Church, Warrington.

MEMORIALS
St Elphin's Church, Warrington; Spion Kop (Spioenkop), KwaZulu-Natal, South Africa (1st Battalion); Queen's Gardens, Palmyra Square, Warrington (South African War).

BATTLE HONOURS
Louisburg, Martinique 1762, Havannah, St Lucia 1778, Monte Video, Rolica, Vimiero, Corunna, Talavera, Badajoz, Salamanca, Vittoria, Pyrenees, Nivelle, Orthes, Toulouse, Peninsula, Niagara, Waterloo, Candahar 1842, Ghuznee 1842, Cabool 1842, Maharajpore, Sevastopol, Lucknow, New Zealand, Relief of Ladysmith, South Africa, 1899–1902, Baluchistan 1918, Afghanistan 1919.

The 1st Battalion, The South Lancashire Regiment's final charge at Pieters Hill during the Relief of Ladysmith in 1900. From a painting by W. B. Wollen.

Mons, Ypres 1914 '15 '17 '18, Aisne 1914 '18, Messines 1914 '17 '18, Somme 1916 '18, Lys, Doiran 1917 '18, Sari Bair, Baghdad.

Dunkirk 1940, Normandy Landing, Bourguebus Ridge, Falaise, Rhineland, North West Europe 1940 '44–5, Madagascar, North Arakan, Kohima, Nyaungu Bridgehead.

LATER LINEAGE

Amalgamated in 1958 with The East Lancashire Regiment as The Lancashire Regiment. In 1970 The Lancashire Regiment was amalgamated with The Loyal Regiment (North Lancashire) as The Queen's Lancashire Regiment.

MUSEUMS

Museum of The Queen's Lancashire Regiment, Fulwood Barracks, Preston, Lancashire PR2 8AA (telephone: 01772 260362; fax: 01772 260583). Additional items are displayed in *The Museum of Lancashire*, Old Sessions House, Stanley Street, Preston, Lancashire PR2 9WL (telephone: 01772 264075) and *Warrington Museum*, Bold Street, Warrington, Cheshire WA1 1JG (telephone: 01925 442392; website: www.warrington.gov.uk).

The Manchester Regiment
(63rd and 96th Foot)

ORIGINS AND DEVELOPMENT

The 63rd was raised in 1758 from the 2/8th Foot and was affiliated to west Suffolk in 1782. The 96th was raised in Manchester in 1824. In 1881 they were linked as the 1st and 2nd Battalions, The Manchester Regiment. Reduced to a single battalion in 1948. Amalgamated 1958.

HISTORY

The 63rd was active in the American War of Independence, being present at Bunker Hill and at the capture of both New York and Charleston. It even served as mounted infantry during the campaign for the southern colonies under the command of the talented British partisan leader Banastre Tarleton. The 96th inherited a sphinx badge for 'Egypt' and the battle honour 'Peninsula' from the four earlier disbanded creations of the 96th dating back to 1761. One of the latter had been known as both The Queen's German Regiment and The Minorca Regiment between 1798 and 1818. In 1872 the 63rd and 96th were twinned, with their permanent base at Ashton-under-Lyne barracks, built between 1843 and 1845 in reaction to Chartist-inspired civil unrest in the northern mill towns. In the South African War, the 1st Battalion helped drive back the major Boer assault on Ladysmith on 6th January 1900, holding a key position at Caesar's Camp. In the First World War, the regiment raised forty-two battalions. On 21st March 1918 Lieutenant Colonel Wilfred Elstob, with the 16th Battalion, held 'Manchester Hill' near St Quentin, as he had promised, 'to the last'. Elstob won a posthumous Victoria Cross. In 1942 a small party of the 1st Battalion was sent away from Singapore to become the nucleus of a new battalion, but they, too, were captured. Consequently, the 6th Battalion was renumbered the 1st to preserve the traditions of the regular battalion. Out of 1003 men in Singapore, only 460 returned to Britain: sixty died in action and the remainder in Japanese captivity.

VICTORIA CROSSES

South African War (2); First World War (11); Mesopotamia, 1920 (1). Of these,

The Colours of The Manchester Regiment in Manchester Cathedral and the regiment's South African war memorial.

five are in the Regimental Museum.

NICKNAMES

The Bloodsuckers (63rd): from the fleur-de-lis badge of the 63rd, said to resemble deadly West Indian mosquitoes.

The Bendovers (96th): from the possibility of reversing the digits 6 and 9.

The Upside Downers (96th): as above.

BADGE

The Arms of the City of Manchester were borne as the badge in 1881 but, in 1923, the regiment reverted to a plain fleur-de-lis, the badge of the old 63rd, which had been awarded in 1759 for service at the capture of Guadaloupe in the West Indies from the French, whose Royal emblem it was.

MOTTO

Concilio et labore ('By council and labour').

FACINGS

Deep green (63rd).
Yellow (96th).
White (Manchester Regiment).

REGIMENTAL MARCHES

'The Young May Moon' (63rd).

73

'The Manchester' (96th).
'Farewell Manchester' (slow march).

COLOURS
Manchester Cathedral.

MEMORIALS
Ardwick Green, Manchester; Whitworth Park, Manchester; St Ann's Square, Manchester; All Saints Church, Trimulgherry, India; Caesar's Camp, Ladysmith and Elandslaagte, KwaZulu-Natal, South Africa (1st Battalion); Contalmaison Communal Cemetery, Somme (12th Battalion, 1914–18), Montauban (16th, 17th, 18th and 19th Battalions – 1st City Pals Brigade), France.

BATTLE HONOURS
Guadaloupe 1759, Egmont-op-Zee, Peninsula, Martinique 1809, Guadaloupe 1810, New Zealand, Alma, Inkerman, Sevastopol, Afghanistan 1879–80, Egypt 1882, Defence of Ladysmith, South Africa 1899–1902.
Mons, Givenchy 1914, Ypres 1915 '17 '18, Somme 1916 '18, Hindenburg Line, Piave, Macedonia 1915–18, Gallipoli, Megiddo, Baghdad.
Dyle, Defence of Arras, Caen, Scheldt, Lower Maas, Roer, Reichswald, Gothic Line, Malta 1940, Kohima.

LATER LINEAGE
Amalgamated in 1958 with The King's Regiment (Liverpool) as The King's Regiment (Manchester and Liverpool). In 1969 this became The King's Regiment.

MUSEUMS
The Museum of the Manchester Regiment, Ashton Town Hall, The Market Place, Ashton-under-Lyne, Tameside, Manchester OL6 6DL (telephone: 0161 343 2878 or 0161 342 3078 or 0161 342 3710; website: www.tameside.gov.uk).

LEICESTERSHIRE

The Royal Leicestershire Regiment
(17th Foot)

ORIGINS AND DEVELOPMENT

The 17th was raised in London in 1688 as Richards' Regiment. It was affiliated to Leicestershire in 1782, becoming The Leicestershire Regiment in 1881. The Royal title was awarded in 1946. A 2nd Battalion existed from 1858 to 1948. The regiment became the 4th Battalion, The Royal Anglian Regiment in 1964.

HISTORY

The 17th's first duty was guarding Windsor Castle in the last troubled days before King James II fled to France. Seven years later, the regiment took part in the capture of the French fortress of Namur on the junction of the Meuse and the Sambre, during which 104 men were killed, including the commanding officer. The regiment took part in the Spanish campaign during the War of Spanish Succession, distinguishing itself at Almanza on 27th April 1707. While acting as flank guard to the British camp at Princeton on 3rd January 1777, the 17th attacked a greatly superior force of George Washington's troops, capturing an artillery battery and then successfully breaking out of encirclement to return to the British lines. Serving as reminders of the regiment's service in the American War of Independence are badges and buttons recovered from later archaeological excavations on building sites in New York. Between 1804 and 1823 the regiment spent eighteen years in India, seeing service in Bundelkund in 1807, on the Sutlej in 1808 and against the Gurkhas of Nepal between 1813 and 1814. A silver snuffbox represents the only piece of the mess silver to be recovered from the wreck of the troopship *Hannah* in 1840. Two Russian cannon were taken at Sevastopol in September 1855 and presented to the City of Leicester by the regiment three years later. In 1899 the 1st Battalion was sent from India to reinforce the British garrison of Natal, taking part in the first action of the South African War at Talana Hill on 20th October 1899 and being caught up in the subsequent siege of Ladysmith. In March 1915 the 2nd Battalion distinguished itself at Neuve Chapelle in the first major British offensive on the Western Front, while the 1/4th Battalion played a leading part in the attack on the Hohenzollern Redoubt at Loos on 15th September 1915. The 2nd Battalion was later the first to enter Baghdad on 11th March 1917 during the British advance up the Tigris. In 1940 the 1/5th Battalion was in the disastrous Norwegian campaign, conducting a fighting retreat to Andalsnes where it was evacuated by the Royal Navy. The 2nd Battalion was also to be evacuated by sea, this time from Crete, where it fought desperately to defend Heraklion from German airborne forces on 20th May 1941. After the war, the 1st Battalion was in Korea and was also the last British battalion to serve in the Sudan before its independence in 1956.

VICTORIA CROSSES

Crimean War (1); First World War (3). Of these, two are in the Regimental Museum.

NICKNAMES

The Tigers: from the badge.
Lily Whites: from the white facings.

BADGE

The Royal Tiger badge with 'Hindoostan' was awarded in 1823 for its service in India, especially that against the Marathas. A laurel wreath surrounding the tiger on the regimental collar badge was awarded by King George III for the 17th's gallantry at Princeton.

MOTTO

Honi soit qui mal y pense ('Let him who thinks evil of it be ashamed').

CUSTOMS

The 17th was another regiment whose officers wore a black line in their lace to commemorate the death of James Wolfe at Quebec. The band would also play a few bars of *Wolfe's Lament* when the regiment was on parade, while all ranks stood to attention. On guest nights in the officers' mess, a black crepe ribbon was laid the length of the dining table. The award of the Tiger badge by King George IV on 25th June 1823 was celebrated every year on the nearest weekend.

FACINGS

White.

REGIMENTAL MARCHES

'A Hunting Call'.

'General Monckton 1762' (slow march).

COLOURS

St Martin's Cathedral Church, Leicester. Many are in store and it is intended that they will be buried in a casket in the Cathedral.

MEMORIALS

Intombi, Ladysmith, KwaZulu-Natal, South Africa (1st Battalion). A unique memorial is land purchased at Bagworth in the National Forest in 1993 and planted with trees representing countries in which the regiment served.

BATTLE HONOURS

Namur 1695, Louisburg, Martinique 1762, Havannah, Ghuznee 1839, Khelat, Afghanistan 1839, Sevastopol, Ali Masjid, Afghanistan 1878–9, Defence of Ladysmith, South Africa 1899–1902.

Aisne 1914 '18, Neuve Chapelle, Somme 1916 '18, Ypres 1917, Cambrai 1917 '18, Lys, St Quentin Canal, France and Flanders 1914–18, Palestine 1918, Mesopotamia 1915–18.

Scheldt, North West Europe 1944–5, Sidi Barrani, North Africa 1940–1 '43, Salerno, Gothic Line, Italy 1943–5, Crete, Malaya 1941–2, Chindits 1944.

LATER LINEAGE

The 4th Battalion, The Royal Anglian Regiment was absorbed into the other three battalions of The Royal Anglian Regiment in 1970.

MUSEUMS

The Royal Tigers Gallery, New Walk Museum, 53 New Walk, Leicester LE1 7EA (telephone: 0116 255 4900; website: www.leicestermuseums.ac.uk).

Bren gun carriers of The Leicestershire Regiment training 'somewhere in Scotland' in January 1941.

The 2nd Battalion, The Lincolnshire Regiment, arrives at Lincoln from Catterick for a Trooping the Colour ceremony in 1935.

LINCOLNSHIRE

The Royal Lincolnshire Regiment
(10th Foot)

ORIGINS AND DEVELOPMENT

The 10th was raised in 1685 as Grenville's Regiment, being affiliated to North Lincolnshire in 1782. In 1881 it became The Lincolnshire Regiment, receiving its Royal title in 1946. A 2nd Battalion existed from 1858 to 1948. Amalgamated 1960.

HISTORY

The 10th originated in an independent company raised by the Earl of Bath to assist in the suppression of the Duke of Monmouth's rebellion against King James II in 1685. Early service was in Flanders, with the regiment seeing its first action at Steenkirk on 3rd August 1692. It was present at all of Marlborough's victories. In the American War of Independence, the 10th fought at Bunker Hill, Brandywine and Germantown, returning to England for the first time in nearly fifty years in 1779. Sent to Egypt from India in 1801, the regiment marched 120 miles (193 km) across the desert from Kosseir on the Red Sea coast to Keneh on the Nile to participate in the battle at Alexandria on 21st March 1801. Both the 1/10th and the 2/10th fought in the Peninsular War. The regiment was in India again during the Sikh Wars, especially distinguishing itself at Sobraon on 10th February 1846, when it advanced in absolute silence and perfect order on the Sikh entrenchments. It was also present at Mooltan and Goojerat in the Second Sikh War and remained in India during the Mutiny. Indeed, it made a gallant attempt to relieve the Europeans surrounded in a small house at Arrah in July 1857, taking heavy casualties. As it sailed home from Calcutta, the governor general ordered the guns of Fort William to be fired in salute. In 1898 the 1st Battalion was on the Nile for the reconquest of the Sudan, being present at Omdurman on 2nd September 1898 when fifty thousand dervishes were repulsed by massed firepower at a cost of only twenty-five British, Egyptian and Sudanese fatalities. The battalion went to the aid of Hector 'Fighting Mac' Macdonald's Sudanese brigade at a critical moment. During the First World War, a detachment from the Bermuda Rifle Volunteer Corps was attached to the 1st Battalion. The 10th Battalion, known as the 'Grimsby Chums', took 502 casualties out of 842 men engaged at La Boiselle on 1st July 1916. Three battalions were at Loos in September 1915, while six were involved in the successful assault on the Hindenburg Line in September 1918. Both the 2nd and the 6th Battalions were evacuated from Dunkirk in 1940, while the 4th was evacuated from Norway. Subsequently, the 2nd and 4th Battalions served in North West Europe in 1944–5, while the 6th fought in North Africa and Italy and the 1st in Burma, taking part in both Arakan campaigns in 1943 and 1944.

VICTORIA CROSSES

Indian Mutiny (3); First World War (3); Second World War (1). Of these, three are in the Regimental Museum.

NICKNAMES

The Yellow Bellies: from the yellow ground of the first Colours and the original yellow facings.

The Poachers: from the popular song (and regimental march).

BADGE
The Sphinx and 'Egypt' was awarded for service in Egypt in 1801.

MOTTO
Honi soit qui mal y pense ('Let him who thinks evil of it be ashamed').

CUSTOMS
In 1881 the regiment should have changed its regimental Colour to a white ground, reflecting the official change of its facing from yellow to white. In the event, by repairing Colours presented to the regiment in 1859 and 1863, The Lincolns avoided changing to a white ground until well into the twentieth century. Following service together at Sobraon in February 1846, The Lincolns and The Worcestershire Regiment played each other's regimental marches before their own on ceremonial occasions.

FACINGS
White.

REGIMENTAL MARCHES
'The Lincolnshire Poacher'.

COLOURS
Lincoln Cathedral.

MEMORIALS
Lincoln Cathedral; St Mathias's Church, Lincoln; Haartebeespoort Dam, Rietfontein and Silkaatsnek, South Africa (2nd Battalion); St James's Church, Grimsby (10th Battalion, 1914–18).

BATTLE HONOURS
Blenheim, Ramillies, Oudenarde, Malplaquet, Peninsula, Sobraon, Mooltan, Goojerat, Punjaub, Lucknow, Atbara, Khartoum, Paardeburg, South Africa 1900–02.
Mons, Marne 1914, Messines 1914 '17 '18, Ypres 1914 '15 '17, Neuve Chapelle, Loos, Somme 1916 '18, Lys, Hindenburg Line, Suvla.
Dunkirk 1940, Normandy Landing, Fontenay le Pesnil, Antwerp–Tournhout Canal, Rhineland, North Africa 1943, Salerno, Gothic Line, Ngakyedauk Pass, Burma 1943–5.

LATER LINEAGE
Amalgamated in 1960 with The Northamptonshire Regiment as the 2nd East Anglian Regiment (Duchess of Gloucester's Own Royal Lincolnshire and Northamptonshire). In 1964 this became the 2nd Battalion, The Royal Anglian Regiment. This four-battalion regiment was reduced to three battalions in 1970 and to two in 1992.

MUSEUMS
The Royal Lincolnshire Regiment Museum, The Museum of Lincolnshire Life, Burton Road, Lincoln LN1 3LY (telephone: 01522 528448; website: www.lincolnshire.gov.uk).

LONDON

The Royal Fusiliers (City of London Regiment) (7th Foot)

ORIGINS AND DEVELOPMENT

The 7th Foot was raised in 1685 as The Ordnance Regiment or Royal Regiment of Fuzileers to garrison the Tower of London. It was affiliated to Derbyshire in 1782. In 1881 it became The Royal Fusiliers (The City of London Regiment). A 2nd Battalion existed from 1858 to 1948. In 1968 the regiment became the 3rd Battalion, The Royal Regiment of Fusiliers.

HISTORY

The Tower of London was the army's ordnance store, hence the original alternative title of the 7th. Previously, grenadier companies had been armed with the short flintlock carbine or 'fusil', which was also then given to those designated as escorts to the guns since the lighted matches necessary for matchlocks were too dangerous to use in proximity to gunpowder. Since the 7th as a whole were ordnance guards, they became Fusiliers, though losing the title in 1782 and not regaining it until 1881. During the War of Spanish Succession, the regiment was part of the small garrison of Lérida in Spain, which was granted the honours of war by the French when finally forced to surrender on 12th November 1707. In the American War of Independence, one of the Colours was taken by the Americans at Fort Chamblé in 1775 during their advance on Montreal and is now on display at West Point. One officer of the 7th in North America was Major John André, captured by the Americans on 23rd September 1780 while acting as a go-between with the American general, Benedict Arnold, who intended to defect to the British and arrange the surrender of West Point. Though wearing his uniform under a greatcoat when taken, André was controversially executed as a spy. In the Napoleonic Wars the 1/7th and 2/7th, together with the 23rd Foot (later The Royal Welch Fusiliers), successfully stormed the commanding French position at Albuhera on 16th May 1811, an action that led the force to be famously described by the military historian Sir William Napier as 'that astonishing infantry'. An eagle had also been taken from the French 82nd Regiment at the capture of Martinique on 30th January 1809. In 1904 four companies of the 1st Battalion were together the largest British component of the expeditionary force to Tibet under Colonel Sir Francis Younghusband. Of the Victoria Crosses on display in the Tower are the first two and the last two awarded in the First World War. At Nimy railway bridge over the Mons canal, Lieutenant Maurice Dease and Private Frank Godley won theirs on 23rd August 1914, holding back the German advance with a machine gun. Dease died of his wounds while the badly wounded Godley was captured, but not before throwing the gun into the canal. Privates Samuel Pearce and Arthur Sullivan won their Victoria Crosses in North Russia in 1919, where British forces were committed to assist the White Russian armies against the Bolsheviks in an early phase of the Russian Civil War (1917–21). At Monte Cassino in Italy the 1st and 2nd Battalions served alongside each other in 1943–4. After consolidation in 1948, the 1st Battalion saw active service in Korea in 1950–1.

VICTORIA CROSSES

Crimean War (5); Second Afghan War (1); South African War (1); First World War (11); North Russia, 1919 (2). Of these, eleven are in the Regimental Museum.

NICKNAMES
The Elegant Extracts: from the drafting in of aristocratic officers from other units when the regiment was raised in 1685.

BADGE
The Bursting Grenade was associated with all Fusilier regiments, commemorating the original role in protecting artillery. The White Rose of York is contained by the Garter within the grenade.

MOTTO
Honi soit qui mal y pense ('Let him who thinks evil of it be ashamed').
Nec aspera terrent ('Hardship has no terrors for us').

CUSTOMS
To mark the regiment's links with the City of London, from 1924 its regular battalions had the privilege of marching through the City with drums beating, Colours flying and bayonets fixed. Previously, the privilege had been accorded only the 4th (Territorial) Battalion, which traced its own origins to the Tower Hamlets Regiments of the London Trained Bands. The bandsmen carried brass hilted swords and scabbards presented by the Duke of Kent, the father of Queen Victoria, who was appointed colonel of the regiment in 1789. In the pre-1939 full-dress and the post-1945 No. 1 dress, the red stripe worn on the overalls (trousers) of the officers was wider than that of other infantry regiments in order to mark the regiment's origins as artillery guards, since the wider stripe was also worn by the Royal Artillery. Having been presented with a silver wine cooler by King William IV in 1836, the regiment was also absolved by the king from drinking the Loyal Toast.

FACINGS
Royal blue.

REGIMENTAL MARCHES
'The British Grenadiers'.
'Fighting with the 7th Royal Fusiliers'.
'Die Normandie' (slow march).

COLOURS
St Sepulchre's Church, Fleet Street; St Michael's Church, Cornhill; St Edmund's Church, Lombard Street; Warlingham Parish Church, Surrey; St Ann's Church, Manchester; Winchester Cathedral; the National Army Museum; the United States Military Academy, West Point.

MEMORIALS
Holborn Bars, High Holborn;

The Royal Fusiliers memorial at Holborn Bars, London.

81

Fusilier House, Balham; the Guildhall, City of London; Warlingham, Surrey; St Symphonien Cemetery, Mons, Belgium; Pretoria, South Africa (2nd Battalion); Windmill Hill, Gibraltar (road construction, 1842).

BATTLE HONOURS

Namur 1695, Martinique 1809, Talavera, Busaco, Albuhera, Badajoz, Salamanca, Vittoria, Pyrenees, Orthes, Toulouse, Peninsula, Alma, Inkerman, Sevastopol, Kandahar 1880, Afghanistan 1879–80, Relief of Ladysmith, South Africa 1899–1902.

Mons, Ypres 1914 '15 '17 '18, Nonne Bosschen, Somme 1916 '18, Arras 1917 '18, Cambrai 1917 '18, Hindenburg Line, Struma, Landing at Helles, Egypt 1916.

Dunkirk 1940, Keren, North Africa 1940, 1943, Mozzagrogna, Salerno, Garigliano Crossing, Anzio, Cassino II, Gothic Line, Cariano, Korea 1952–3.

LATER LINEAGE

In 1992 the 3rd Battalion, The Royal Regiment of Fusiliers, was absorbed into the 1st and 2nd Battalions.

MUSEUMS

The Fusiliers Museum, Her Majesty's Tower of London, London EC3N 4AB (telephone: 020 7488 5610; fax: 020 7481 1093; website: www.army.mod.uk/ceremonialandheritage/museums).

The Royal Regiment of Fusiliers on patrol duty in Cyprus c.1990.

MIDDLESEX

The Middlesex Regiment (Duke of Cambridge's Own)
(57th and 77th Foot)

ORIGINS AND DEVELOPMENT

The 57th was raised in 1755 and was affiliated to west Middlesex in 1782. The 77th was raised in 1787 for service in India, becoming affiliated to east Middlesex in 1807. In 1876 it was named The Duke of Cambridge's Own Regiment, the Duke then being the army's commander-in-chief. In 1881 they were linked as the 1st and 2nd Battalions, The Duke of Cambridge's Own (Middlesex Regiment). In 1921 it was renamed The Middlesex Regiment (Duke of Cambridge's Own) and, in 1948, following amalgamation of the two battalions, the new single-battalion regiment was known as The 57th/77th Middlesex Regiment (Duke of Cambridge's Own). Regular 3rd and 4th Battalions existed between 1900 and 1922. The regiment became The 4th Battalion, the Queen's Regiment in 1966.

HISTORY

The 57th embarked almost immediately after being raised for marine service in the Mediterranean. In the American War of Independence it served under Lord Cornwallis from 1775 to 1783, its actions including the battle of Brooklyn, the capture of York island and the storming of Port Montgomery. Its most celebrated action, however, was at Albuhera in the Peninsula on 16th May 1811, where 428 of the 570 men who went into action became casualties while holding a vital hill against French attack. The regiment continued to serve through the remaining significant actions of Wellington's campaign. In India the 77th took part in the capture of Cananore and, in 1790, in the Mysore campaign against the notorious Tippoo Sahib. Renewed hostilities on the part of Tippoo saw the regiment engaged in the siege of his fortress at Seringapatam. The regiment then returned to Europe and it, too, took part in the Peninsular War, being one of the three regiments detailed to lead the storming of the breach at Ciudad Rodrigo on 19th January 1812. The 4th Battalion distinguished itself at Mons on 23rd August 1914, while the 2nd Battalion succeeded in breaking into the German front line at Neuve Chapelle on 10th March 1915. An interesting memorial to the stand at Mons is that erected by the Germans for the 'Royal' Middlesex Regiment since they apparently could not believe that such gallantry would be displayed by an ordinary line regiment. During the Second World War, the 1st Battalion was part of the small garrison of Hong Kong that held out against overwhelming odds for seventeen days before being forced to surrender on 25th December 1941. A former commanding officer serving on the Hong Kong staff, Colonel Newnham, was tortured by the Japanese for seventeen days and then executed after he refused to divulge any information. Later, being shipped to Japan itself on the *Lisbon Maru*, the survivors of the battalion were locked in the holds when it was torpedoed by an allied submarine on 2nd October 1942. Lieutenant Colonel Stewart prevented panic and organised the breaking down of the hatches, saving 170 men, but he himself died a few days later from his exertions. In June 1950 the 1st Battalion was among the first British units to reach Korea and, despite containing a high proportion of young national servicemen, performed extremely well, winning seven battle honours, of which two were placed on the Colours.

VICTORIA CROSSES

Crimean War (4); Third Maori War (2); First World War (5). Of these, three are

83

The 57th at Albuhera.

displayed at Dover and four in the National Army Museum.

NICKNAMES

The Diehards: from Albuhera when the wounded Colonel William Inglis rallied his men, calling out, 'Die hard, my men, die hard!' or, in some versions, 'Die hard, 57th, die hard!'. The call was to be echoed by Captain E. Stanley of the 77th at Inkerman on 5th November 1854 and by Second Lieutenant R. P. Hallowes, VC of the 4th Battalion, killed at Bellewaarde Ridge on 30th September 1915.

The Pot Hooks (77th): from the figure seven.

BADGE

The Ostrich Plumes and *Ich Dien* motto of the Prince of Wales was awarded to the 77th in 1810. The Coronet and Cipher are those of the Duke of Cambridge.

MOTTO

Ich Dien ('I serve').

FACINGS

Yellow.

REGIMENTAL MARCHES

'Sir Manley Power'(quick march, 59th).

'Paddy's Resource' (quick march, 77th).

'Daughter of the Regiment' (slow march).

'The Caledonian March' (slow march, 57th).

'The Lass O'Gowrie' (march past).

'The Garb of Old Gaul' (2nd Battalion).

84

COLOURS
St Paul's Cathedral.

MEMORIALS
St Paul's Cathedral; Canterbury Cathedral; Inglis Barracks, Mill Hill; St Paul's Church, Mill Hill; St Mary's Church, Hornsey; All Hallows' Church, Tottenham; St Leonard's Church, Shoreditch; St Nicholas's Church, Chiswick; Chipping Barnet Parish Church; Stoke-on-Trent Parish Church; St Symphonien Cemetery, Mons, Belgium (1914).

BATTLE HONOURS
Mysore, Seringapatam, Albuhera, Ciudad Rodrigo, Badajoz, Vittoria, Pyrenees, Nivelle, Nive, Peninsula, Alma, Inkerman, Sevastopol, New Zealand, South Africa 1879, Relief of Ladysmith, South Africa 1900–02.
Mons, Marne 1914, Ypres 1915 '17 '18, Albert 1916 '18, Bazentin, Cambrai 1917 '18, Hindenburg Line, Suvla, Jerusalem, Mesopotamia 1917–18.
Dunkirk 1940, Hong Kong, El Alamein, Akarit, Sicily 1943, Anzio, Normandy Landing, Caen, Mont Pincon, The Rhine, Korea 1950–51, Naktong Bridgehead.

LATER LINEAGE
The 4th Battalion, The Queen's Regiment was reduced to company strength in 1970 and placed in abeyance (disbanded) in 1973.

MUSEUMS
The Regimental Collection of the Middlesex Regiment is in the care of the *National Army Museum*, Royal Hospital Road, Chelsea, London SW3 4HT (telephone: 020 7730 0717; website: www.national-army-museum.ac.uk). Items are displayed throughout the museum, but a special case devoted to the regiment is also located on the museum's top-floor corridor. Additional items are displayed in *The Princess of Wales's Royal Regiment and Queen's Regiment Museum*, Dover Castle, Dover, Kent CT16 1HU (telephone: 01227 818053; website: www.army.mod.uk/ceremonialandheritage/museums).

NORFOLK

The Royal Norfolk Regiment
(9th Foot)

ORIGINS AND DEVELOPMENT

The 9th Foot was raised as Cornwall's Regiment in 1685, becoming affiliated to east Norfolk in 1782. In 1881 it became The Norfolk Regiment, receiving the Royal title in 1935. A 2nd Battalion existed from 1857 to 1948. Amalgamated 1959.

HISTORY

Raised by King James II to secure his throne, the regiment's first action was against James at the Boyne in 1690. In the eighteenth century it saw much service in the Caribbean. Forced to surrender with the rest of John Burgoyne's army at Saratoga in October 1777, the regiment's Colours were hidden by Lieutenant Colonel Hill to prevent capture and were later presented to the king on the regiment's return to England. Soldiers of the 9th buried Sir John Moore after his death in the victory at Corunna on 16th January 1809, which enabled the army to escape by sea. Arriving in India in 1835, the regiment took part in the First Afghan War and the First Sikh War (1845–6), winning battle honours for Moodkee, Ferozeshah and Sobraon. It served also in the Second Afghan War and, later, on the British expedition into Tibet in 1903–4. At Gallipoli on 12th August 1915 the 1/5th Battalion attacked Turkish positions around Tekke Tepe, just two days after landing. Having received conflicting orders, what has become known as the 'vanished' battalion, which contained a company partly recruited from the Royal estate at Sandringham, advanced beyond support and was surrounded and slaughtered. The men's unmarked graves were discovered in 1919, leading to continuing speculation over their actual fate. During the retreat to Dunkirk, men of the 2nd Battalion were massacred by German *Schutzstaffel* troops at Le Paradis on 26th May 1940, while the 7th Battalion was captured at St Valéry-en-Caux while serving alongside the 51st (Highland) Division on 12th June 1940. Similarly, the 4th, 5th and 6th Battalions had the misfortune of being captured by the Japanese at Singapore. In winning five Victoria Crosses in the Second World War, however, the Norfolks won more than any other British regiment. One was earned by Captain John Randle of the 2nd Battalion at Kohima on 4th May 1944 for single-handedly charging a Japanese machine-gun bunker that was pinning down his men. Mortally wounded, Randle threw himself across the bunker's firing slit.

VICTORIA CROSSES

First World War (1); Second World War (5). Of these, two are displayed in the Regimental Museum.

NICKNAMES

The Holy Boys: from the mistaken belief by the Spanish in the Peninsular War that the regiment's badge represented the Virgin Mary.

The Fighting Ninth: from the regimental number.

BADGE

The exact reason for the adoption of the distinctive Britannia badge is unknown but, traditionally, it was said to have been awarded by Queen Anne for service at Almanza in 1707, being officially confirmed in 1799.

MOTTO
Honi soit qui mal y pense ('Let him who thinks evil of it be ashamed').

CUSTOMS
Following the regiment's part at Corunna, the drummers wore black braids in commemoration of Sir John Moore.

FACINGS
Yellow.

REGIMENTAL MARCHES
'Rule Britannia'.

COLOURS
Norwich Cathedral; Sandringham Church.

MEMORIALS
Norwich Cathedral; Canterbury Cathedral; St George's Chapel, Windsor.

BATTLE HONOURS
Belleisle, Havannah, Martinique 1794, Rolica, Vimiero, Corunna, Busaco, Salamanca, Vittoria, St Sebastian, Nive, Peninsula, Cabool 1842, Moodkee, Ferozeshah, Sobraon, Sevastopol, Kabul 1879, Afghanistan 1879–80, Paardeburg, South Africa 1900–02.
Mons, Le Cateau, Marne 1914, Ypres 1914 '15 '17 '18, Somme 1916 '18, Hindenburg Line, Landing at Suvla, Gaza, Shaiba, Kut al Amara 1915 '17.
St Omer-La Bassee, Normandy Landing, Brioux Bridgehead, Venraij, Rhineland, North West Europe 1940 '44–5, Singapore Island, Kohima, Aradura, Burma 1944–5, Korea 1951–2.

LATER LINEAGE
Amalgamated in 1959 with The Suffolk Regiment as the 1st East Anglian Regiment (Royal Norfolk and Suffolk). In 1964 it became the 1st Battalion, The Royal Anglian Regiment. This four-battalion regiment was reduced to three battalions in 1970 and to two in 1992.

MUSEUMS
Royal Norfolk Regimental Museum, Shirehall, Market Avenue, Norwich, Norfolk NR1 3JQ (telephone: 01603 493650; website: www.norfolk.gov.uk /tourism/museums/regi.htm).

St Saviour's Chapel in Norwich Cathedral has panelling displaying the achievements of The Royal Norfolk Regiment.

NORTHAMPTONSHIRE

The Northamptonshire Regiment
(48th and 58th Foot)

ORIGINS AND DEVELOPMENT

The 48th was raised at Norwich in 1741 as Cholmondeley's Regiment and the 58th at Plymouth in 1755. In 1782 the 48th was affiliated to Northamptonshire and the 58th to Rutland. In 1881 they became the 1st and 2nd Battalions, The Northamptonshire Regiment. Reduced to a single battalion in 1948. Amalgamated 1960.

HISTORY

Raised for the War of Austrian Succession, the 48th initially served in Flanders but was recalled during the Jacobite incursion, occupying Edinburgh and then being present at Falkirk on 17th January 1746 and standing firm alongside the 4th Foot (The King's Own) when several other regiments gave way. It was one of two regular regiments despatched to North America in 1755, participating in the advance on Fort Duquesne by Major-General Edward Braddock, which led to the famously disastrous ambush of the force by the French and their Indian allies on the Monongahela on 9th July 1755. One result was the raising of eleven new regiments, including what was to become the 58th. The 48th and the 58th were to serve alongside each other in the successful expedition in 1758 to seize the fortress of Louisburg, which commanded the mouth of the St Lawrence. In the following year, both were present at the battle of the Heights of Abraham before Quebec, a surgeon of the 48th attending the dying James Wolfe. The 48th spent long periods in the West Indies during the remainder of the eighteenth century, while the 58th was at Gibraltar from 1779 to 1783, being awarded the Castle and Key emblem for its services during the Great Siege and later the Sphinx badge for its part in the Egypt campaign of 1801. Both the 48th (now with two battalions) and the 58th served in the Peninsular War, the 1/48th particularly distinguishing itself on 27th–28th July 1809 at Talavera, where, in Wellington's words, 'the battle was saved by its advance and steady conduct'. In the Victorian era the 48th besieged Sevastopol in the Crimea and the 58th fought in the First Maori War in 1845–7, which was followed by the Zulu War of 1879. At Laing's Nek on 26th January 1881, during the First Boer War, the 58th had the distinction of being the last British regiment to carry its Colours into action. When Lieutenant Baillie was wounded Lieutenant Peel carried both Colours until he was tripped up by an ant-bear hole and rendered unconscious. Believing Peel dead, a sergeant then carried the Colours to safety while Baillie was rescued under fire by Lieutenant Hill, who won the Victoria Cross. The lessons learnt by the 58th fighting the Boers in this war, and by the 2nd Battalion in the Second Boer War of 1899–1902, led to the regiment becoming one of the finest shooting regiments in the army, winning many competitions, and devising field tactics and march disciplines adopted by the rest of the infantry. The 1st Battalion, meanwhile, had had its first experience of North West Frontier operations in the Tirah expedition of 1897–8. In the First World War the 1st Battalion went through the Retreat from Mons in 1914 and later, with the 2nd Battalion, lost heavily at Aubers Ridge on 9th May 1915. Both battalions remained on the Western Front, being joined there by the 5th, 6th and 7th Battalions, while the 4th served at Gallipoli and Palestine. During the inter-war years the 1st Battalion was the first infantry battalion ever to be transported by air, from Egypt to Iraq in 1932 to guard Royal Air Force airfields. This was followed by further North West Frontier

The 58th Foot was the last regiment to carry its colour into battle, at Laing's Nek in 1881.

operations in 1936 against the Fakir of Ipi. In the Second World War the 1st Battalion garrisoned India until 1943, when it went to the Burma Campaign until VJ day (15th August 1945). Meanwhile, the 2nd and 5th Battalions served in the 1940 campaign in France, later fighting in Madagascar (2nd), North Africa (5th), Sicily and Italy (both battalions).

VICTORIA CROSSES
First Boer War (2); First World War (6); Second World War (1). Of these, three are held in the Regimental Museum.

NICKNAMES
The Black Cuffs (58th): from the original black facings.
The Steelbacks (58th): supposedly from the fortitude of the 58th in the Peninsular War, caring 'as little for flogging as for the Frenchman's steel'.
The Four and Eights (48th): from the regimental number.
The Cobblers (48th): from the chief industry of Northampton.

BADGE
The Castle and Key is that of Gibraltar, earned by the 58th during the great siege

of 1779–83. 'Talavera' was awarded to the 48th for the role of the 1/48th at the anchor point of Wellington's line. While several other regiments received the battle honour, only the 48th was allowed to display it on its badges, buttons and insignia.

MOTTO
Montis insignia Calpe ('The insignia of Gibraltar is the Rock').

CUSTOMS
Talavera Day was particularly celebrated each year, the toast 'To the 48th' being drunk in the officers' mess. Between 1881 and 1948 it remained the custom for the regiment always to refer to the 1st and 2nd Battalions as the 48th and 58th. In speech and writing 'Northamptonshire' was always abbreviated to 'Northamptons', never to 'Northants'.

FACINGS
White from 1881 (in common with all non-Royal English regiments), but from 1927 the 48th's buff was restored for full dress and officers' mess dress.

REGIMENTAL MARCHES
'The Northamptonshire' (48th).
'The Lincolnshire Poacher' (quick march, originally 58th).
'The Duchess' (slow march).

COLOURS
Church of the Holy Sepulchre, Northampton. The Colours of the 58th borne at Laing's Nek, formerly in the National Army Museum, are now in the Regimental Museum.

MEMORIALS
Church of the Holy Sepulchre, Northampton; Peterborough Cathedral; Regimental Museum; Laing's Nek, KwaZulu-Natal, South Africa; English cemetery at Elvas, Portugal, for Badajoz and Albuera.

BATTLE HONOURS
Louisburg, Quebec 1759, Martinique 1762, 1794, Havannah, Gibraltar, Maida, Egypt, Duoro, Talavera, Albuera, Badajoz, Salamanca, Vittoria, Pyrenees, Nivelle, Orthes, Toulouse, Peninsula, New Zealand, Sevastopol, South Africa 1879, Tirah, Modder River, South Africa 1899–1902.
Mons, Marne 1914, Aisne 1914 '18, Ypres 1914 '17, Neuve Chapelle, Loos, Somme 1916 '18, Arras 1917 '18, Epehy, Gaza.
North West Europe 1940–45, North Africa 1942–3, Italy 1943–5, Garigliano Crossing, Anzio, Cassino II, Yu, Imphal, Myinmu Bridgehead, Burma 1943–5.

LATER LINEAGE
Amalgamated in 1960 with The Royal Lincolnshire Regiment as The 2nd East Anglian Regiment (Duchess of Gloucester's Own Royal Lincolnshire and Northamptonshire). In 1964 this became the 2nd Battalion, The Royal Anglian Regiment. This four-battalion regiment was reduced to three battalions in 1970 and to two in 1992.

MUSEUMS
Regimental Museum of The Northamptonshire Regiment, Abington Park Museum, Park Avenue South, Northampton NN1 5LW (telephone: 01604 838110).

NORTHUMBERLAND

The Royal Northumberland Fusiliers
(5th Foot)

ORIGINS AND DEVELOPMENT

The 5th Foot was raised for the Dutch service in 1674 as 'Clare's Irish Regiment' and was taken on in the English establishment in 1685. In 1782 it was affiliated to Northumberland. It was converted to a fusilier role in 1836 and became the Northumberland Fusiliers. It received its Royal title in 1935. A 2nd Battalion existed from 1857 to 1948. In 1968 it became the 1st Battalion, The Royal Regiment of Fusiliers.

HISTORY

After joining the English establishment, the regiment served in Ireland in 1690 and at the siege of Namur in 1695, before seeing service in the Spanish campaign during the War of Spanish Succession. In the Seven Years War, the regiment participated in a number of amphibious operations and then took the surrender of a French regiment at Kirch Denkern in 1761. Wilhelmstahl on 24th June 1762 became a unique battle honour borne only by the regiment, which defeated a much larger French grenadier regiment during this victory by the Marquis of Granby over the French in Silesia. As a result, the 5th was allowed to wear French-style grenadier caps. The Wilhelmstahl snuff box was also presented to the regiment's commanding officer, Lieutenant Colonel Marly, by Prince Ferdinand of Brunswick, in whose cause Granby's army fought the battle. A company of the regiment took part in the first engagement of the American War of Independence at Lexington and Concord on 19th April 1775, forming the rearguard during the retreat back to Boston. The 5th served as marines in the West Indies in 1778, hence the adoption of 'Rule Britannia' as a regimental march and of the white hackle for its part in defeating a

The 5th Foot at the Battle of Wilhelmstahl in 1762, a unique battle honour borne by The Royal Northumberland Fusiliers.

The Northumberland Fusiliers photographed after the action at St Eloi in March 1916.

force of reinforcements landed to restore the French position on the island of St Lucia. In the Peninsular War, the 2/5th distinguished itself at El Bodon, dispersing a cavalry force by charging it. The regiment had only garrison service for forty-two years following the defeat of Napoleon, but, in the Indian Mutiny, it was part of the relieving force led by Sir James Outram, which fought its way into Lucknow but was then itself besieged. In the South African War, the 2nd Battalion was involved in the British defeat at Stormberg in Cape Colony on 10th December 1899, one of the three defeats of 'Black Week', the others being Colenso and Magersfontein. On 1st July 1916, the 20th, 21st, 22nd and 23rd Battalions, comprising the Tyneside Scottish Brigade, suffered grievous casualties at La Boiselle on the Somme, losing seventy officers and 2440 men, including all four commanding officers and every officer and non-commissioned officer in one battalion. In the Second World War the 1st Battalion served in North Africa, including at the defence of Tobruk; the 2nd in Italy and Greece; the 4th in the North West Europe campaigns of 1940 and 1944; and the 9th lost at Singapore when part of the 18th Division tragically landed almost at the end with virtually no chance to fight before the surrender. After the war the regiment served in Korea and Kenya before a trying period of service in Aden in 1967.

VICTORIA CROSSES
   Indian Mutiny (3); First World War (5); Second World War (2). Of these, five are in the Regimental Museum.

NICKNAMES
   The Shiners: from their smart turn-out at a parade in Ireland in 1769.
   The Old and Bold: from Rolica in the Peninsular War.
   The Fighting Fifth: from the regimental number, and supposedly coined by Wellington.
   Wellington's Bodyguard: from the Peninsular War, when the regiment acted as a guard to Wellington's headquarters one summer.

BADGE
   The Order of the Garter emblem of St George and the Dragon mounted on a Grenade, the latter being to commemorate the original role of fusiliers in protecting artillery.

MOTTO
Quo fata vocant ('Whither the fates call').

CUSTOMS
St George's Day (23rd April) was kept with particular ceremony, the drums and head-dresses of all ranks being decked with red and white roses and a special 'Wilhelmstahl or Drummer's Colour', a gosling green silk banner, being paraded. The property of the officers of the regiment, this Colour appeared officially only on this day each year. In the old full dress, a fusilier cap with scarlet and white hackle was worn, the custom of wearing white feathers having been begun as a result of the 5th defeating a much larger French force on St Lucia in 1778 and taking the white feathers from the Frenchmen's head-dress. In 1829 William IV ordered the red-over-white plume to be worn only by the regiment, 'As a peculiar mark of honour whereby its former service will still be commemorated'. At the time, the rest of the infantry were to wear a white plume.

FACINGS
Gosling green, which was preserved even after the regiment became a Royal one.

REGIMENTAL MARCHES
'The British Grenadiers'.
'Rule Britannia'.
'Blaydon Races'.

COLOURS
St Nicholas's Cathedral, Newcastle; St Mary's Church, Newcastle; St Mary's Church, Alnwick.

MEMORIALS
St Nicholas's Cathedral, Newcastle; St Mary's Church, Newcastle; Barras Bridge, Newcastle (Commercials Battalion, First World War); St Mary's Church, Alnwick; Kerksdorp and Krugersdorp, South Africa (1st and 2nd Battalions).

BATTLE HONOURS
Wilhelmstahl, St Lucia 1778, Rolica, Vimiero, Corunna, Busaco, Ciudad Rodrigo, Badajoz, Salamanca, Vittoria, Nivelle, Orthes, Toulouse, Peninsula, Lucknow, Afghanistan 1879–80, Khartoum, Modder River, South Africa 1900–02.
Mons, Marne 1914, Ypres 1914 '15 '17 '18, St Julien, Somme 1916 '18, Scarpe 1917 '18, Selle, Piave, Struma, Suvla.
Dunkirk 1940, Caen, Rhineland, Sidi Barrani, Defence of Tobruk, Tobruk 1941, Cauldron, El Alamein, Salerno, Cassino II, Imjin, Korea 1950–1.

LATER LINEAGE
A four-battalion regiment at its creation, The Royal Regiment of Fusiliers was reduced to three battalions in 1969 and to two in 1992.

MUSEUMS
The Fusiliers Museum of Northumberland, The Abbot's Tower, Alnwick Castle, Alnwick, Northumberland NE66 1NG (telephone: 01665 602152; website: www.northumberlandfusiliers.org.uk).

NOTTINGHAMSHIRE

The Sherwood Foresters (Nottinghamshire and Derbyshire Regiment) (45th and 95th Foot)

ORIGINS AND DEVELOPMENT

The 45th Foot was raised in 1741 and was affiliated to Nottinghamshire in 1782. The 95th was raised in 1823 and affiliated to Derbyshire in 1825. The 45th received the title of Sherwood Foresters in 1866. The two regiments were linked as the 1st and 2nd Battalions, The Sherwood Foresters (Derbyshire Regiment) in 1881. In 1902 Nottinghamshire was added to the title. Amalgamated 1970.

HISTORY

The 45th saw its first service in North America, being present at the siege of Louisburg in 1758 and the capture of Quebec in the following year. It then served in home stations but spent three lengthy periods in the West Indies between 1778 and 1801, suffering considerable losses from yellow fever. At Badajoz on 6th April 1812, men of the 45th formed part of a volunteer storming party. Corporal James Talbot of the 45th was one of only two soldiers in the army to earn fifteen out of the twenty-nine clasps available for the Military General Service Medal, covering campaigns between 1793 and 1814, when it was issued in 1847. Amid the long years of political and socio-economic unrest that followed the end of the Napoleonic Wars, the 45th provided the troops at the so-called 'Battle of Bossenden Wood' in Kent on 31st May 1838, when eleven followers of the self-styled 'Sir William Courtenay' (also known as John Toms) died in a farcical attempted insurrection. The 95th saw its first serious action in the Crimea, capturing a set of Russian drums at the Alma on 20th September 1854, an action in which Captain MacDonald was saved by a bullet hitting the ornament on his cross belt. In 1888, as the 2nd Battalion, it took part in the Sikkim campaign on India's Northeastern frontier, resisting Tibetan influence and eventually campaigning at over 12,600 feet (3840 metres). Some thirty-three battalions were raised during the First World War,

the 2/5th Battalion taking part in the suppression of the Easter Rising in Dublin in April 1916. One famous member of the regiment was General Sir Horace Smith-Dorrien. Commissioned in the 95th in 1877, he commanded II Corps in 1914–15, saving the British Expeditionary Force as a whole by his stand at Le Cateau on 26th August 1914. Captain Albert Ball VC initially served with the 1/7th (Robin Hood) Battalion, before transferring to the Royal Flying Corps in 1916. One of Britain's leading 'aces', Ball was killed on 7th May

General Sir Horace Lockwood Smith-Dorrien GCB GCMG DSO, Colonel of The Sherwood Foresters 1905–30.

94

1917. Relics on display include his Victoria Cross, flying gloves, watch, and parts of some of his aircraft such as a windscreen pierced by a bullet.

VICTORIA CROSSES
Indian Mutiny (1); Dargai, 1897 (1); South African War (2); First World War (8); Second World War (1). Of these, nine are in the Regimental Museum in addition to that of Captain Albert Ball, VC.

NICKNAMES
The Old Stubborns (45th): from its role in the Peninsular War.
Nottingham Hosiers (45th): from the Nottingham hosiery trade.
The Nails (95th): from its steadfastness in battle during the Crimean War.

BADGE
The White Hart and Oak-leaves mounted on a Maltese Cross are allusions to Sherwood Forest.

MOTTO
Honi soit qui mal y pense ('Let him who thinks evil of it be ashamed').

CUSTOMS
At Badajoz, Lieutenant Macpherson of the 45th in the absence of a Union Flag hoisted his jacket on the French flagpole to signal that the breach attack had been successful. In the annual celebration of the event, therefore, a red jacket was hoisted on the regimental flagstaffs and at Nottingham Castle. To commemorate the capture of the Russian drums at the Alma, the 95th had its own drums edged with black and white triangles in imitation of the Russian fashion. In the same battle, casualties were so heavy that a private soldier had to carry the Queen's Colour, with the result that at the annual celebration of Alma Day the Colour was henceforth entrusted to the longest serving private soldier. During the Mutiny, the 95th found a ram tethered in a temple yard at Kotah on 30th March 1858. It was released and remained with the regiment through about 3000 miles (almost 5000 km) of marching and six actions in central India and, named Private Derby, was awarded the Mutiny Medal. A ram mascot was kept by the regiment thereafter, led on parade by the Ram Major

*Private
Derby XII.*

'Bravo, Torr Top!

This part of New Mills is famed forever by giving its
name to one of the hottest parts of the battle line in France.
In Torr Top Street there is a winner of the Distinguished
Conduct Medal and a winner of the Military Medal, whilst
in the little street below the Torr Top Mission there is another winner
of the Distinguished Conduct Medal and another winner of the
Military Medal. All honour to Torr Top! Where in England is there
another place so small in area which has so distinguished itself in the war?
Torr Top should be enshrined in the hearts of New Mills people!
Torr Top, above all other places, should be made a place fit for heroes to live'
High Peak Reporter 1919

Corporal John Cooper of Torr Top Street joined the Sherwood Foresters in
1914. He served in France throughout the war. He was both gassed and
wounded. Corporal Cooper was awarded the DCM 'for Distinguished
Conduct in the field'. But he had another claim to fame for it was he
who gave the name Torr Top to a trench in the Ypres area.
The name was printed on a board and appeared on the official
Military Map. Following the Armistice the board, splattered
still with the mud of Flanders, was presented to the town.

TORR TOP
TUNNELS

*At New Mills, Derbyshire, is Torr Top, where
this monument commemorates Corporal John
Cooper DCM of The Sherwood Foresters, and
the famous Torr Top trench at Ypres.*

and Ram Orderly in its scarlet coat with Lincoln-green facings, and bearing a replica of the Mutiny medal and a silver forehead plate. The tradition is kept up in the Worcestershire and Sherwood Foresters Regiment, Private Derby XXVII having been presented by the Duke of Devonshire in 1999. The Duke's Swaledale herd at Chatsworth provided all but three of the rams in the twentieth century.

FACINGS
    Lincoln green.

REGIMENTAL MARCHES
    'The Young May Moon'.
    'I'm Ninety Five'.
    'The Derby Ram'.

COLOURS
    Derby Cathedral; the Parish Churches of Ilkeston, Bakewell, Chesterfield, Edensor, Newark and Mansfield; Regimental Museum, Nottingham Castle.

MEMORIALS
    Crich Hill, Derbyshire.

BATTLE HONOURS
    Louisburg, Rolica, Vimiero, Talavera, Busaco, Fuentes d'Onoro, Ciudad Rodrigo, Badajoz, Salamanca, Vittoria, Pyrenees, Nivelle, Orthes, Toulouse, Peninsula, Ava, South Africa 1846–7, Alma, Inkerman, Sevastopol, Central India, Abyssinia, Egypt 1882, Tirah, South Africa 1899–1902.
    Aisne 1914 '18, Neuve Chapelle, Loos, Somme 1916 '18, Ypres 1917 '18, Cambrai 1917 '18, St Quentin Canal, France and Flanders 1914–18, Italy 1917–18, Gallipoli 1915.
    Norway 1940, Gazala, El Alamein, Tunis, Salerno, Anzio, Campoleone, Gothic Line, Coriano, Singapore Island.

LATER LINEAGE
    Amalgamated in 1970 with The Worcestershire Regiment to form The Worcestershire and Sherwood Foresters Regiment (29/45th Foot).

MUSEUMS
    The Sherwood Foresters (45th and 95th Regiments) Museum, Nottingham Castle Museum and Art Gallery, Nottingham NG1 6EL (telephone: 0115 915 3700). Additional items are displayed in *Derby City Museum and Art Gallery*, The Strand, Derby DE1 1BS (telephone: 01332 293111) and *Newark Museum*, Appletongate, Newark, Nottinghamshire NG22 1JY (telephone: 01636 655740) (8th Battalion).

OXFORDSHIRE

The Oxfordshire and Buckinghamshire Light Infantry
(43rd and 52nd Foot)

ORIGINS AND DEVELOPMENT

The 43rd was raised at Winchester in 1741 and the 52nd at Coventry in 1755. In 1782 the 43rd was affiliated to Monmouthshire and the 52nd to Oxfordshire. In 1881 they were linked as the 1st and 2nd Battalions, The Oxfordshire Light Infantry. In 1908 the regiment was renamed The Oxfordshire and Buckinghamshire Light Infantry. Reduced to a single battalion in 1948. In 1966 it became the 1st Battalion, The Royal Green Jackets.

HISTORY

Both the 43rd and the 52nd began their existence as the 54th Foot before being renumbered as a consequence of others' disbandment. The 43rd garrisoned Minorca before proceeding to North America in 1757, where it took a prominent part in the capture of Quebec two years later. Service followed in the West Indies. The 52nd was also sent to North America in 1765. Both served in the American War of Independence, fighting side by side at Lexington and Bunker Hill; the 43rd was part of Lord Cornwallis's army forced to surrender at Yorktown on 19th October 1781. The 43rd and 52nd were the first two regiments selected for experimental training as light infantry at Shorncliffe Camp in 1803 under the command of Sir John Moore. Joined by the 95th Rifles, they were formed into the famous Light Brigade. Both took part in Moore's retreat to Corunna in January 1809. Returning to Portugal, the brigade accomplished the remarkable feat of marching 250 miles (402 km) to the battlefield of Talavera, the last 42 miles (68 km) in just twenty-six hours in the hottest weather of the year. Subsequently formed into a Light Division with the addition of the Chestnut Troop, Royal Horse Artillery and two Portuguese battalions, the 43rd and 52nd distinguished themselves throughout the Peninsular War. Among relics of Sir John Moore are a diamond star presented by officers of the 52nd when he received the Order of the Bath, and the sash used to lower his body into the grave at Corunna. At Waterloo on 18th June 1815, the 52nd played a decisive role when Sir John Colborne led his men in a flank charge against the French Imperial Guard at the climax of the battle. Sent to Canada, the 43rd made another notable march in December 1837, covering 370 miles (595 km) in eighteen days in the depths of winter to confront a revolt by the so-called 'Sons of Liberty'. The 52nd distinguished itself in the storming of the Kashmir Gate in Delhi on 14th September 1857, Bugler Hawthorne winning the Victoria Cross for sounding the advance under intense fire as charges blew in the gate, and then rescuing an injured engineer officer. During the First World War the 1st Battalion took heavy casualties at Ctesiphon before Baghdad on 22nd November 1915 and then suffered the subsequent siege of Kut, the garrison of which was compelled to surrender to the Turks on 29th April 1916 after five months. Only ninety men survived captivity. Meanwhile, the 2nd Battalion achieved fame at Nonne Bosschen on 11th November 1914, routing the Prussian Potsdam Guards at a crucial phase in the First Battle of Ypres. In the Second World War the 2nd Battalion was selected for glider training. On the night of 5th–6th June 1944, the task of Major John Howard's D Company of the battalion, as part of 6th Airborne Division, was to seize what became known as 'Pegasus Bridge', over the Caen Canal, and 'Horsa Bridge', over the Orne River, and to hold them until relieved by troops advancing from the Normandy beaches.

After the war, the 1st Battalion served against EOKA terrorists on Cyprus 1956–9, in the Brunei revolt in 1962 and through the beginning of the Confrontation between Malaysia and Indonesia.

VICTORIA CROSSES

Indian Mutiny (3); Third Maori War (1); First World War (2). Of these, four are displayed at Winchester.

NICKNAMES

The Light Bobs: from their role as light infantry in the Peninsula in the Light Division under the command of Robert 'Black Bob' Craufurd – as compared to their own supposedly jollier outlook.

BADGE

The Bugle with Strings, denoting light infantry.

MOTTO

Honi soit qui mal y pense ('Let him who thinks evil of it be ashamed').

FACINGS

White.

REGIMENTAL MARCHES

'Nach Flager Von Grenada' (43rd).
'Lower Castle Yard' (52nd).

The memorial at Paardeburg to men of The Oxfordshire Light Infantry killed during the South African War.

'The Italian Song' (4th Battalion).

COLOURS
Christ Church, Oxford.

MEMORIALS
Slade Park, Headington (South African War); Rose Hill, Oxford; Gruisbank Cemetery, Paardeburg, Orange Free State, and Jacobsdal, South Africa (1st Battalion).

BATTLE HONOURS
Quebec 1759, Martinique 1762, Havannah, Mysore, Hindoostan, Martinique 1794, Vimiero, Corunna, Busaco, Fuentes d'Onoro, Ciudad Rodrigo, Badajoz, Salamanca, Vittoria, Pyrenees, Nivelle, Nive, Orthes, Toulouse, Peninsula, Waterloo, South Africa 1851–2–3, Delhi 1857, New Zealand, Relief of Kimberley, Paardeburg, South Africa 1900–02.

Mons, Ypres 1914 '17, Langemarck 1914 '17, Nonne Bosschen, Somme 1916 '18, Cambrai 1917 '18, Piave, Doiran 1917 '18, Ctesiphon, Defence of Kut al Amara.

Cassel, Ypres-Comines Canal, Normandy Landing, Pegasus Bridge, Reichswald, Rhine, Enfidaville, Salerno, Anzio, Gemmano Ridge.

LATER LINEAGE
The three-battalion regiment of The Royal Green Jackets formed in 1966 also comprised the former King's Royal Rifle Corps (2nd Battalion) and The Rifle Brigade (3rd Battalion). It was reduced to two battalions in 1992.

MUSEUMS
Museum of the Oxfordshire and Buckinghamshire Light Infantry, Slade Park, Headington, Oxford OX3 7JL (telephone: 01865 780128; website: www.army.mod.uk/ceremonialandheritage/museums). Additional items are displayed in *The Royal Green Jackets Museum*, Peninsula Barracks, Romsey Road, Winchester, Hampshire SO23 8TS (telephone: 01962 828459; website: www.army.mod.uk/ceremonialandheritage/museums).

RUTLAND
(see **Northamptonshire**)

SHROPSHIRE

The King's Shropshire Light Infantry (KSLI)
(53rd and 85th Foot)

ORIGINS AND DEVELOPMENT

The 53rd was raised in 1755 and affiliated to Shropshire in 1782. The 85th was raised in Buckinghamshire in 1793 as The Bucks Volunteers, two earlier regiments having previously had the number in 1759 and 1779. It was converted to light infantry in 1809 and in 1814 was designated The Duke of York's Own Regiment of Light Infantry as a result of its services in the Peninsular War and the Anglo-American War of 1812–14. In 1821 it became The King's Light Infantry after guarding King George IV during a riot at Brighton. In 1881 they were linked as the 1st and 2nd Battalions, The King's Shropshire Light Infantry. Reduced to a single battalion in 1948. In 1968 the regiment became the 3rd Battalion, The Light Infantry.

HISTORY

Raised by Colonel William Whitmore of Apley, near Bridgnorth, the 53rd proceeded to North America in 1775, seeing its first major actions in the American War of Independence. It then served in the Flanders campaign in 1793–4, earning the battle honour 'Nieuport' shared only with the Royal Marines. The 85th was part of the British force that burned the presidential mansion in Washington in 1814. Subsequently, when the building was restored, it became known as the White House since white paint was used to obscure the scorch marks. Relics of the 85th include the Colour taken from the James City Light Infantry and the Guidon of the Harford Dragoons, both captured from the Americans at Bladensburg outside Washington on 24th August 1814. The 85th earned the motto *Aucto splendore resurgo* ('I rise again with increased splendour') from its distinguished conduct after the earlier disbandment of the previous regiments bearing the number 85th in 1763 and 1782. The 53rd was in India from 1804 to 1823 and again during the Sikh Wars, guarding the famous Koh-i-noor Diamond, which was subsequently incorporated into the Crown Jewels. The regiment also possesses a lock of Napoleon's hair, acquired by Captain Poppleton of the 53rd while acting as orderly officer to the exiled emperor on St Helena. There are also relics of General Viscount Hill, a divisional commander under Wellington and later commander-in-chief of the army, who served in the 53rd as a subaltern. In 1894 the 1st Battalion was in Hong Kong when plague struck. For the battalion's work in burying the dead and disinfecting housing, each officer received a gold medal and each enlisted man a silver medal from the Hong Kong authorities. In the South African War the 2nd Battalion travelled some 6000 miles (almost 10,000 km) with the 19th Brigade, taking part in ten general actions and twenty-seven minor actions in five months. The regiment had eight battalions in service during 1914–18. At Bligny on 6th June 1918 the 1/4th Battalion made a crucial counter-attack to re-establish the line against the Germans, winning the French Croix de Guerre. In the Second World War Corporal Priday of the 1st Battalion had the misfortune to be the first British soldier killed in action. After the war, the regiment fought in Korea and against the Mau Mau in Kenya between 1955 and 1957.

VICTORIA CROSSES

Indian Mutiny (5); First World War (1); Second World War (2). Of these, three are in the Regimental Museum.

The King's Shropshire Light Infantry, 1865–1912, showing a variety of uniforms and headgear worn by private soldiers, musicians and officers between those years.

The King's Shropshire Light Infantry in 'cold weather' kit with cardigans on the North West Frontier, India 1930.

NICKNAMES

    The Brickdusts (53rd): from the original red facings.

    The Young Bucks (85th): to distinguish itself from the Old Bucks (16th Foot).

    The Old Five and Threepennies (53rd): from the regimental number.

BADGE
The Bugle with strings of the light infantry and the 'KSLI' monogram.

MOTTO
Aucto splendore resurgo ('I rise again in greater splendour').

CUSTOMS
According to tradition the Loyal Toast was not drunk in the officers' mess, supposedly because King George IV had said that no further demonstration of loyalty was required from the 85th after its service to him in Brighton in 1821, a riot being occasioned by the mob's support for the king's estranged queen, Caroline of Brunswick, when he attended the Theatre Royal.

FACINGS
Royal blue.

REGIMENTAL MARCHES
'The Farmer's Boy'.
'Old Towler (1st Battalion)'.
'Daughter of the Regiment' (2nd Battalion).

COLOURS
Regimental Museum, Shrewsbury; The Quarry, Shrewsbury; St Mary's Church, Shrewsbury; St Chad's Church, Shrewsbury; St Leonard's Church, Bridgnorth.

MEMORIALS
The Quarry, Shrewsbury; St Mary's Church, Shrewsbury; St Chad's Church, Shrewsbury; St Mary's Church, Pembroke; St John's Church, Pembroke Dock; Suakin, Sudan; Belfast, South Africa (1st Battalion).

BATTLE HONOURS
Nieuport, Tournay, St Lucia 1796, Talavera, Fuentes d'Onoro, Salamanca, Vittoria, Pyrenees, Nivelle, Nive, Toulouse, Peninsula, Bladensburg, Aliwal, Sobraon, Goojerat, Punjaub, Lucknow, Afghanistan 1879–80, Egypt 1882, Suakin 1885, Paardeburg, South Africa 1899–1902.
Armentières 1914, Ypres 1915 '17, Frezenberg, Somme 1916, Arras 1917 '18, Cambrai 1917 '18, Bligny, Epehy, Doiran 1917 '18, Jerusalem.
Dunkirk 1940, Normandy Landing, Antwerp, Venraij, Hochwald, Bremen, North West Europe 1940 '44–5, Tunis, Anzio, Italy 1943–5, Kowang-San, Korea 1951–2.

LATER LINEAGE
Initially a four-battalion regiment, The Light Infantry was subsequently reduced to three battalions in 1969 and to two in 1993.

MUSEUMS
The Shropshire Regimental Museum, The Castle, Shrewsbury, Shropshire SY1 2AT (telephone: 01743 262292).

SOMERSET

The Somerset Light Infantry (Prince Albert's) (13th Foot)

ORIGINS AND DEVELOPMENT

The 13th was raised in 1685 as the Earl of Huntingdon's Regiment, becoming affiliated to Somerset in 1782. The regiment became light infantry in 1822 and was rewarded with the title Prince Albert's Regiment of Light Infantry for its defence of Jellalabad in 1842. It became Prince Albert's (Somersetshire Light Infantry) in 1881; Prince Albert's (Somerset Light Infantry) in 1912; and, finally, The Somerset Light Infantry (Prince's Albert's) in 1921. A 2nd Battalion existed from 1858 to 1948. Amalgamated 1959.

HISTORY

Another of the regiments raised for King James II, the 13th saw its first action at Killicrankie in Scotland in 1689 in the service of King William III. During the War of Spanish Succession the regiment served for seven years in Spain, being mounted as Pearce's Dragoons. It was at Dettingen, Fontenoy and Culloden. The sphinx superscribed 'Egypt' was awarded for service with Abercrombie at Aboukir Bay in 1801 and was borne on the Colours. After serving in Canada, the regiment participated in the First Burma War (1824–6). Perhaps the best-known episode in the 13th's history was its defence of Jellalabad in the First Afghan War in 1842. Left there while the main British army marched on to Kabul, it was besieged when that army was destroyed, the news being carried back to the city on 13th January 1842 by the sole survivor of the retreating army to break through, Dr Brydon. The 'Illustrious Garrison' held out for three months until it made a sortie and defeated an Afghan force of six thousand men a week before the arrival of General Pollock's relief force, greeted by the 13th's band playing *Oh! but ye've been lang o'coming!*. The 2/13th, raised in 1858, saw service in the Third Burma War (1885–7) and the South African War. The 1/13th was in Zululand, one of its members winning a Victoria Cross in the retreat down the Devil's Pass at Hlobane on 27th March 1879. On the following day, the battalion participated in the major defeat of the Zulus at Khambula, which marked the turning point in the war. Of the nineteen battalions of the regiment during the First World War, eleven served overseas. The 2nd Battalion remained in India throughout but participated in the Third Afghan War (1919). During the Second World War the 1st Battalion initially served on the North West Frontier, continuing the inter-war operations against recalcitrant tribesmen in Waziristan. The 2nd Battalion garrisoned Gibraltar and then served in Italy, while the 10th Battalion was converted to the 7th (Light Infantry) Battalion, The Parachute Regiment and took part in the airborne assault in the early hours of D-Day. In 1947 the 1st Battalion was the last British regiment to leave India by marching through the 'Gateway of India' in Bombay. In 1952 the regiment's most distinguished member, Field Marshal the Lord Harding, became Chief of the Imperial General Staff.

VICTORIA CROSSES

Indian Mutiny (2); Zulu War (1); First World War (1); Second World War (1). Of these, three are in the Regimental Museum.

NICKNAMES

The Illustrious Garrison: from the defence of Jellalabad.

The Jellalabad Heroes: as above.

BADGE

The Mural Crown, superscribed 'Jellalabad', was awarded for the defence of Jellalabad. The Bugle is that of all light infantry while the cipher within the strings is that of Prince Albert.

MOTTO

Honi soit qui mal y pense ('Let him who thinks evil of it be ashamed').

CUSTOMS

Sergeants of the 13th wore their sashes over the left shoulder instead of the right, traditionally said to commemorate the battle of Culloden on 16th April 1746 when most of the officers became casualties and the non-commissioned officers took command. The practice was not actually authorised officially until 1865.

FACINGS

Royal blue, worn, despite the 13th not being a Royal regiment, as a further distinction for its defence of Jellalabad.

REGIMENTAL MARCHES

'Prince Albert'.

COLOURS

Regimental Museum, Taunton; St Mary's Church, Taunton; Bath Abbey; the Minster, Ilminster; Burrington Church.

MEMORIALS

St Mary's Church, Taunton; Taunton Town Centre (Burma War); Bath Abbey; the Minster, Ilminster; Burrington Church; Canterbury Cathedral (First Afghan War); Wells Cathedral (Zulu War); Khambula (1st Battalion) and Wynne Hill, Tugela Heights (2nd Battalion), KwaZulu-Natal, South Africa.

BATTLE HONOURS

Gibraltar 1704–5, Dettingen, Martinique 1809, Ava, Ghuznee, Afghanistan 1839, Cabool 1842, Sevastopol, South Africa 1878–9, Burma 1885–7, Relief of Ladysmith, South Africa 1899–1902, Afghanistan 1919.

Marne 1914 '18, Aisne 1914, Ypres 1915 '17 '18, Somme 1916 '18, Albert 1916 '18, Arras 1917 '18, Cambrai 1917 '18, Hindenburg Line, Palestine 1917–18, Tigris 1916.

Hill 112, Mont Pincon, Rhineland, Rhine, North West Europe 1944–5, Cassino II, Cosina Canal Crossing, Italy 1944–5, North Arakan, Ngakyedauk Pass.

LATER LINEAGE

Amalgamated in 1959 with The Duke of Cornwall's Light Infantry as The Somerset and Cornwall Light Infantry. In 1968 this became the 1st Battalion, The Light Infantry. This four-battalion regiment was reduced to three battalions in 1969 and to two in 1993.

MUSEUMS

The Somerset Military Museum, 14 Mount Street, Taunton, Somerset TA1 3QE (telephone: 01823 333434; fax: 01823 351639).

STAFFORDSHIRE

The North Staffordshire Regiment (The Prince of Wales's) (64th and 98th Foot)

ORIGINS AND DEVELOPMENT

The 64th was raised from the 2/11th Foot in 1759 and was affiliated to Staffordshire in 1782 as the 2nd Staffordshire. The 98th was raised in 1824. In 1876 it was given the title of The Prince of Wales's. In 1881 the two were linked as the 1st and 2nd Battalions, The North Staffordshire Regiment (The Prince of Wales's). Reduced to a single battalion in 1949. Amalgamated 1959.

HISTORY

The 64th spent much of its early existence in the West Indies or North America between 1759 and 1803 and then served in India. Indeed, the absence of any European battle honours until the First World War is unique among English county regiments. It did, however, gain honours for service in Martinique and St Lucia while in the West Indies and earned 'Surinam' in 1804 for taking two Dutch forts and thus opening the way for the capture of New Amsterdam in this South American colony. In 1842 ten companies of the 64th were on board the troopship *Alert* when it hit rocks off Nova Scotia. To keep the vessel on an even keel until it could be beached, the men stood in their ranks below deck, the water up to their knees. The 98th, meanwhile, was serving in the First China War, earning a Red Dragon badge superscribed 'China'. At the time, the commanding officer was Colin Campbell, Lord Clyde, who won national fame leading the 'Thin Red Line' at Balaclava and went on to become commander-in-chief in India during the Mutiny. The regiment possesses the robes, swords, medals, watch and other relics of Campbell, who

commanded the 98th from 1835 to 1847. The 1st Battalion was on the Dongola expedition in 1896, the first phase of Kitchener's re-conquest of the Sudan, while the 2nd Battalion fought in the South African War. Some fifty-two battle honours were won during the First World War. On 31st July 1917 at the opening of the Third Battle of Ypres, popularly known as 'Passchendaele', the 1st Battalion took its objective at great cost while, as part of 46th Division, the Staffordshire Brigade, including 1/6th Battalion, participated in the crossing of the St Quentin Canal on 29th September 1918. The 7th Battalion spearheaded

A stretcher bearer in The North Staffordshire Regiment, Lance Corporal Coltman, VC, DCM and bar, MM and bar, was the most highly decorated soldier of the First World War.

the re-taking of Kut in Mesopotamia in February 1917 while the 2nd Battalion distinguished itself in the Third Afghan War (1919). The 2nd Battalion saw post-war service in the Arab Revolt in Palestine in 1936–9. During the Second World War, the 1st Battalion served in Burma while the 2nd Battalion fought with distinction during the retirement to Dunkirk and also distinguished itself in Tunisia, notably in the attack on Points 151 and 174 on the Jebel Gueriat in April 1943. Landing in the Anzio bridgehead, the battalion was reduced to two-company strength but later fought all the way up Italy to the north of Florence. The amalgamated 1st North Staffords also served in Palestine and Korea.

VICTORIA CROSSES
Indian Mutiny (1); First World War (4). Of these, two are in the Regimental Museum.

NICKNAMES
The Black Knots: from the badge and original facings.

BADGE
As with The South Staffordshire Regiment, the Stafford Knot, but with the addition of the Prince of Wales's Plumes from the 98th.

MOTTO
Ich Dien ('I serve').

FACINGS
White.

REGIMENTAL MARCHES
'The Days we went a-gypsying' (quick march).
'God Bless the Prince of Wales' (slow march).

COLOURS
Garrison Church, Whittington, Lichfield; Lichfield Cathedral.

MEMORIALS
Parish Churches of Stoke-on-Trent and Burton-on-Trent; Garrison Church, Whittington, Lichfield; Lichfield Cathedral; Ecoust-St Mein, Bapaume, France (2/6th Battalion, 1918).

BATTLE HONOURS
Guadaloupe 1759, Martinique 1794, St Lucia 1803, Surinam, Punjaub, Reshire, Bushire, Koosh-ab, Persia, Lucknow, Hafir, South Africa 1900–02, Afghanistan 1919.

Armentières 1914, Somme 1916 '18, Arras 1917, Messines 1917 '18, Ypres 1917 '18, St Quentin Canal, Selle, Sari Bair, Kut al Amara 1917, North West Frontier India 1915.

Dyle, Ypres-Comines Canal, Caen, Brieux Bridgehead, Medjez Plain, North Africa 1943, Anzio, Rome, Marradi, Burma 1943.

LATER LINEAGE
Amalgamated in 1959 with The South Staffordshire Regiment as The Staffordshire Regiment (Prince of Wales's).

MUSEUMS
The Staffordshire Regiment Museum, Whittington Barracks, Lichfield, Staffordshire WS14 9PY (telephone: 0121 311 3229).

The South Staffordshire Regiment
(38th and 80th Foot)

ORIGINS AND DEVELOPMENT
The 38th was raised in Lichfield in 1705 as Lillingstone's Regiment and was affiliated to Staffordshire in 1782. The 80th or Staffordshire Volunteers was raised in the county in 1793. In 1881 the two were linked as the 1st and 2nd Battalions, The South Staffordshire Regiment. Reduced to a single battalion in 1948. Amalgamated 1959.

HISTORY
The 38th spent a record fifty-eight years, from 1707 to 1765, in the West Indies, then one of the unhealthiest stations in the army. Two battle honours were won during this period for service on Guadeloupe in 1759 and Martinique in 1762. The 38th went to North America in 1775, seeing action at Bunker Hill and then garrisoning New York. Some of the 38th returned to the West Indies in the French Revolutionary Wars while others fought in Flanders, as did the 80th, which went overseas within three months of being raised from the Staffordshire militia. Later in

Lance Sergeant Baskeyfield of The South Staffordshire Regiment winning his VC at Arnhem: a painting by Terence Cuneo in the Regimental Museum.

107

The memorial to the men of the 80th Foot killed at Ntombe Drift in Zululand.

the Napoleonic Wars the 38th served extensively in the Peninsula (temporarily raising a second battalion) and the 80th served in Egypt (a sphinx being displayed on the regimental Colour). The 38th served in both the Fifth Kaffir (Cape Frontier) War (1818–19) and the First Burma War (1824–6), also sending a detachment on a punitive expedition to Nicaragua in 1848 before serving in both the Crimea and the Indian Mutiny. The 80th, meanwhile, had undertaken various duties in aid of the civil power in England and convict duty in Australia, being the first British troops sent to New Zealand's South Island. After brief service in the Perak campaign in Malaya in 1875, the 80th went to South Africa. At Intombe (Ntombe) Drift in Zululand on 12th March 1879, the 80th suffered the army's second worst defeat (the worst being at Isandlwana in January). Escorting a wagon convoy, Captain David Moriarty was forced to separate his command when the drift he was attempting to cross began to rise. Moriarty and seventy-one men camped on one side of the drift and Lieutenant Hayward, Sergeant Anthony Booth and thirty-four men on the other. Suddenly attacked by the Zulus in the early hours, Moriarty's party was overwhelmed while Booth conducted a fighting retreat with his party, winning the Victoria Cross. In all, sixty-one soldiers and eighteen civilian drivers were killed. The 80th was avenged when it held the front of the square at the victory of Ulundi. The 38th was subsequently in the same area during the Boer War. In the First World War the 1st Battalion served in Italy, capturing the Austro-Hungarian 38th Regiment in 1918, while the 5th and 6th Battalions took part in the crossing of the St Quentin Canal that same year. In the Second World War the 1st Battalion served with Wingate's Chindits in Burma, while the 2nd Battalion converted to glider troops, spearheading the landing on Sicily in July 1943 and also taking part in the Arnhem operation in September 1944. The amalgamated South Staffords served in the Canal Zone and in Cyprus against EOKA.

VICTORIA CROSSES

Zulu War (2); First World War (3); Second World War (3). Of these, six are in the Regimental Museum.

NICKNAMES

Pump and Tortoise (38th): from the badge.
Staffordshire Knots (38th): from the badge.
Staffordshire Volunteers (80th): from the original title.

BADGE
The Stafford Knot was the ancient badge of the Stafford family. It was worn as a coat-skirt ornament by the 38th from an early stage.

MOTTO
Honi soit qui mal y pense ('Let him who thinks evil of it be ashamed').

CUSTOMS
When the 38th finally returned home after its long years in the West Indies, its regimental clothing was heavily patched with brown cloth, since no new issues of clothing had been received. As a reminder of this, King George V allowed a patch of brown holland to be worn behind the cap badge. To commemorate the battle of Ferozeshah in the First Sikh War on 21st December 1845, the Colours were handed to the Sergeants in recollection of the capture of a Sikh standard by Sergeant Matthew Kirkland of the 38th. The Sikh Colour hangs in Lichfield Cathedral.

FACINGS
White.

REGIMENTAL MARCHES
'Come Lasses and Lads' (quick march).
'The 80th' (slow march).

COLOURS
Garrison Church, Lichfield; Lichfield Cathedral; Walsall Parish Church; Wolverhampton Parish Church.

MEMORIALS
Garrison Church, Lichfield; Lichfield Cathedral; Ntombe Drift, KwaZulu-Natal (80th) and Groenkop, Kestell (1st Battalion), South Africa.

BATTLE HONOURS
Guadaloupe 1759, Martinique 1762, Monte Video, Rolica, Vimiero, Corunna, Busaco, Badajoz, Salamanca, Vittoria, St Sebastian, Nive, Peninsula, Ava, Moodkee, Ferozeshah, Sobraon, Pegu, Alma, Inkerman, Sevastopol, Lucknow, Central India, South Africa 1878–9, Egypt 1882, Kirbekan, Nile 1884–5, South Africa 1900–02.
Mons, Marne 1914, Aisne 1914 '18, Ypres 1914 '17, Loos, Somme 1916 '18, Cambrai 1917 '18, St Quentin Canal, Vittorio Veneto, Suvla.
Caen, Noyers, Falaise, Arnhem 1944, North West Europe 1940 '44, North Africa 1940, Landing in Sicily, Sicily 1943, Chindits 1944, Burma 1944.

LATER LINEAGE
Amalgamated in 1959 with The North Staffordshire Regiment (The Prince of Wales's) as The Staffordshire Regiment (The Prince of Wales's).

MUSEUMS
The Staffordshire Regiment Museum, Whittington Barracks, Lichfield, Staffordshire WS14 9PY (telephone: 0121 311 3229).

SUFFOLK

The Suffolk Regiment
(12th Foot)

ORIGINS AND DEVELOPMENT

The 12th was raised in 1685 as The Duke of Norfolk's Regiment. In 1782 it was affiliated to east Suffolk. In 1881 it became The Suffolk Regiment. A 2nd Battalion existed from 1858 to 1948. Amalgamated 1959.

HISTORY

Raised in response to Monmouth's rebellion, the 12th soon passed into King William III's army, its new Williamite colonel being Henry Wharton, the author of the popular song 'Lilliburlero'. The 12th served in Ireland, hunting the Irish guerrillas known as Rapparees. Transferred to Flanders, it was captured at the fall of Dixmude in 1695 but later exchanged. In the War of Austrian Succession it particularly distinguished itself at Fontenoy in 1745, losing half its manpower as casualties but continuing to fight on through a refusal to believe it could be beaten. The 12th was also one of the six Minden regiments in 1759. Posted to Gibraltar in 1769, the 12th served there throughout the great siege of 1779–83. In the early 1790s it was in Flanders and then went to India, participating in the capture of Tippoo Sultan's fortress at Seringapatam on 4th May 1799. It also took part in the campaign on Mauritius in 1810 and was there again in garrison between 1838 and 1848. One notable episode in the regiment's history was the loss of the troopship *Birkenhead*, which struck a rock off South Africa on 24th February 1852. Among drafts for and families of various regiments were an officer and fifty-five men for the 2/12th, serving in the Eighth Kaffir (Cape Frontier) War. Only three boats could be launched and the men stood fast on the deck while the women and children were put in the boats. Few of the soldiers could swim but none broke ranks to rush the crowded boats. The King of Prussia was so impressed by the discipline shown that he had the story told at the head of every Prussian regiment. The 2nd Battalion was cut off at Le Cateau on 26th August 1914 during the retreat from Mons. Five battalions were involved in the battle of Loos on 25th September 1915. In the Second World War, the 4th and 5th Battalions were lost at Singapore while the 7th was converted into a tank regiment, seeing action in Tunisia and Italy. After the Second World War the 1st Battalion had a highly successful tour of Malaya from 1949 to 1953, accounting for 198 communist guerrillas, before also serving against EOKA terrorists on Cyprus.

VICTORIA CROSSES

First World War (2). Of these, one is in the Regimental Museum.

NICKNAMES

The Old Dozen: from the regimental number.
The Swedebashers: from its rural associations.

BADGE

The Castle and Key of Gibraltar carrying the motto *Montis Insignia Calpe* commemorates defence of the Rock.

MOTTO
Montis Insignia Calpe ('The insignia of Gibraltar is the Rock').

CUSTOMS
'Daffodil Sunday' was the traditional open day of the regiment at Bury St Edmunds.

FACINGS
Yellow.

REGIMENTAL MARCHES
'Speed the Plough'.

COLOURS
St Mary's Church, Bury St Edmunds.

MEMORIALS
St Mary's Church, Bury St Edmunds (including one to those lost on the *Birkenhead*); Luke Copse Cemetery, Serre, Somme, France (2nd Battalion, 1916); Suffolk Hill, Colesberg, South Africa (1st Battalion).

BATTLE HONOURS
Dettingen, Minden, Seringapatam, India, South Africa 1851–2–3, New Zealand, Afghanistan 1878–80, South Africa 1900–02.
Le Cateau, Neuve Chapelle, Ypres 1915 '17 '18, Somme 1916 '18, Arras 1917 '18, Cambrai 1917 '18, Hindenburg Line, Macedonia 1915–18, Landing at Suvla, Gaza.
Dunkirk 1940, Normandy Landing, Odon, Falaise, Venraij, Brinkum, Singapore Island, North Arakan, Imphal, Burma 1943–4.

LATER LINEAGE
Amalgamated in 1959 with The Royal Norfolk Regiment as The 1st East Anglian Regiment (Royal Norfolk and Suffolk). In 1964 it became the 1st Battalion, The Royal Anglian Regiment. This four-battalion regiment was reduced to three battalions in 1970 and to two in 1992.

MUSEUMS
The Suffolk Regiment Museum, The Keep, Gibraltar Barracks, Out Risbygate Street, Bury St Edmunds, Suffolk IP33 3RN (telephone: 01284 752394; website: www.army.mod.uk/ceremonialandheritage/museums).

SURREY

The East Surrey Regiment
(31st and 70th Foot)

ORIGINS AND DEVELOPMENT

The 31st was raised in 1702 as Villier's Marines while the 70th was raised in 1756 in Glasgow from the 2/31st. In 1782 the 31st was affiliated to Huntingdonshire, while the 70th was affiliated to Surrey. The 70th was designated the Glasgow Lowland Regiment from 1813 to 1825. In 1881 they were linked as the 1st and 2nd Battalions, The East Surrey Regiment. Reduced to a single battalion in 1948. Amalgamated 1959.

HISTORY

The 31st remained a marine force until 1714, seeing action at the capture of Gibraltar in 1704 and its subsequent early defence in 1705. Both the 31st and the 70th served in the American War of Independence. Serving on St Lucia between 1796 and 1797, the 31st suffered just fifty-five deaths in action compared to 664 from disease. The 2/31st distinguished itself at Albuhera on 16th May 1811 while the 70th mostly served in the West Indies. Embarked for India in 1825, the 31st was involved in the loss by fire of the East Indiaman, *Kent*, in the Bay of Biscay. Virtually all of the regiment's possessions were lost, including its Colours. A single silver snuff box is all that was recovered of the regiment's mess silver. At Sobraon on 10th February 1846, Sergeant Bernard McCabe of the 31st seized the regimental Colour after its ensign had been killed, and rushed towards the Sikh ramparts, inspiring the men on to victory. Commissioned into the 32nd Foot, McCabe later died of wounds at Lucknow in October 1857 during the Indian Mutiny. In common with The Queen's Royal Regiment (West Surrey), the regiment was one of the recipients of the eight hand-crocheted scarves presented to the army in South Africa by Queen Victoria in 1899. Three Victoria Crosses were won by the 1st Battalion at Hill 60 during the Second Battle of Ypres on 23rd April 1915. Famously, on 1st July 1916, to encourage his men in the 8th (Service) Battalion, Captain W. P. Neville kicked off his company's attack towards Montauban on the Somme across no man's land, having bought a football for each of his four platoons. One was inscribed 'The Great European Cup. The Final. East Surreys v Bavarians. Kick off at Zero'. Neville was killed instantly but the incident was much celebrated in poetry and illustration. Two of the Neville footballs were recovered from the Somme battlefield, one being displayed at Guildford and the other at Dover. During the Second World War, the 2nd Battalion was lost at Singapore: when it surrendered, only 265 men out of 786

One of the footballs kicked 'over the top' by Captain W. P. Neville's Company of The East Surrey Regiment on 1st July 1916 (the first day of the Battle of the Somme).

112

had survived the fighting, and, of these, another 149 were to die in Japanese captivity. Among the Colours in the Regimental Museum are those presented to the 70th by Queen Victoria, which were then carried by the 2nd Battalion and hidden in Singapore in February 1942 to be recovered after the war. After 1945, the 1st Battalion served in the Middle East and was then deployed to Cyprus against EOKA terrorists in 1957.

VICTORIA CROSSES

South African War (1); First World War (7); Second World War (1). Of these, three are in the Regimental Museum's collection.

NICKNAMES

The Young Buffs (31st): from a remark by King George II at Dettingen, having mistaken the 31st for the Buffs (3rd Foot).

The Glasgow Greys (70th): from the original grey facings.

BADGE

The Arms of Guildford on the eight-pointed Star of the Order of the Garter.

MOTTO

Honi soit qui mal y pense ('Let him who thinks evil of it be ashamed').

CUSTOMS

On Sobraon Day (10th February), in commemoration of McCabe, the Colours were always handed to the sergeants' mess for safe keeping. A fragment of the Sobraon Colours was preserved in the lid of a special salt cellar, from which every officer being dined into the mess of the 1st Battalion took salt and then signed a 'Salt Book'. Survivors of the loss of the *Kent*, in 1825, were taken to Chatham and cared for by the Royal Marines. Thereafter, officers of the 31st and the Royal Marines were honorary members of each other's mess. The 31st and, later, the 1st Battalion also followed the Royal Marines' custom of saying Naval Grace before dinner. Officers, the regimental sergeant-major and the bandmaster wore the Royal Marine lanyard. The march 'A Life on the Ocean Wave' would be played on ceremonial occasions. Since the 31st had served as marines themselves, the Loyal Toast was drunk while sitting.

FACINGS

White.

REGIMENTAL MARCHES

'A Southerly Wind and a Cloudy Sky'.
'A Life on the Ocean Wave'.
'Lord Charles Montague's Huntingdonshire March' (slow march).
'The Lass O'Gowrie' (70th).

COLOURS

All Saints' Church, Kingston-on-Thames; Canterbury Cathedral; St Mary's Church, Huntingdon; Regimental Museum.

MEMORIALS

Canterbury Cathedral; St Mary's Church, Huntingdon; Clouston, Colenso, KwaZulu-Natal and Standerton, South Africa (2nd Battalion).

BATTLE HONOURS
Gibraltar 1704–5, Dettingen, Martinique 1794, Talavera, Guadaloupe 1810, Albuhera, Vittoria, Pyrenees, Nivelle, Nive, Orthes, Peninsula, Cabool 1842, Moodkee, Ferozeshah, Aliwal, Sobraon, Sevastopol, Taku Forts, New Zealand, Afghanistan 1878–9, Suakin 1885, Relief of Ladysmith, South Africa 1899–1902.
Mons, Marne 1914, La Bassée 1914, Ypres 1915 '17 '18, Loos, Somme 1916 '18, Albert 1916 '18, Cambrai 1917 '18, Selle, Doiran 1918.
Dunkirk 1940, North West Europe 1940, Qued Zarga, Longstop Hill 1943, North Africa 1942–3, Sicily 1943, Sangro, Cassino, Italy 1943–5, Malaya 1941–2.

LATER LINEAGE
Amalgamated in 1959 with The Queen's Royal Regiment (West Surrey) as The Queen's Royal Surrey Regiment. Became 1st Battalion, The Queen's Regiment in 1966. A four-battalion regiment, The Queen's was reduced to three battalions in 1970. In turn, The Queen's Regiment amalgamated in 1992 with The Royal Hampshire Regiment to form The Princess of Wales's Royal Regiment (Queen's and Royal Hampshires).

MUSEUMS
The Queen's Royal Surrey Regiment Museum, Clandon Park, Guildford, Surrey GU4 7RQ (telephone: 01483 223419; fax: 01483 224636; website: www.surrey-online.uk/queenssurreys). Additional items are displayed in *The Princess of Wales's Royal Regiment and Queen's Regiment Museum*, Dover Castle, Dover, Kent CT16 1HU (telephone: 01304 240121).

The Queen's Royal Regiment (West Surrey) (2nd Foot)

ORIGINS AND DEVELOPMENT
The senior English regiment of Foot, the 2nd was raised as the Tangier Regiment to garrison Tangier in October 1661, this being part of the dowry of King Charles II's queen, Catherine of Braganza. It became The Queen's Regiment in 1684, The Queen Dowager's Regiment in 1686 and The Queen Dowager's Royal Regiment in 1703. Briefly The Princess of Wales's Own Regiment, the 2nd once more became The Queen's Own Royal Regiment in 1727. In 1881 it became The Queen's (Royal West Surrey Regiment) and in 1921 The Queen's Royal Regiment (West Surrey). A 2nd Battalion existed from 1857 to 1948. Amalgamated 1959.

HISTORY
After parading for the first time on Putney Heath under the command of the Earl of Peterborough, the 2nd embarked for Tangier in January 1662, remaining there until it was decided, under financial pressures, to abandon the town in 1684. During the War of Spanish Succession, the regiment won its two mottoes and its Royal title for its conduct at Tongres in 1703 when, with a Dutch regiment, it held a position against overwhelming odds for twenty-eight hours. The regiment won the sphinx for service in Egypt in 1801 but, from 1909, also carried the naval crown on its regimental Colour. This commemorated the service of detachments as marines on board ships of the Royal Navy at the Glorious First of June in 1794, including Admiral Lord Howe's flagship, HMS *Queen Charlotte*. The regiment has one of the eight scarves crocheted in person by Queen Victoria as gifts for soldiers serving in the South African War (1899–1902). There is also a personally knitted scarf and a

Officer's grenadier cap, c.1760, worn by Lieutenant A. Daniel, who served with The Queen's (Second) Regiment of Foot, 1757–70.

wind-cheater jersey presented to members of the regiment by Queen Mary, colonel-in-chief of the regiment from 1937 to 1953, during the Second World War. In the First World War, the Queen's formed thirty-one battalions. Two Empire Gallantry Medals were won by members of the 1st Battalion for rescue work in the aftermath of the Quetta earthquake in India in 1935 while the 2nd Battalion served in the Arab Revolt in Palestine (1936–9). Six Territorial battalions landed at Salerno in Italy on 9th September 1943 as part of 161 and 169 Brigades, the only time when a brigade entirely composed of battalions from a single regiment was relieved in the line by another brigade drawn entirely from the same regiment.

VICTORIA CROSSES
West Africa, 1903 (1); First World War (7); Second World War (1). Of these, two are in the Regimental Museum's collection.

NICKNAMES
Kirke's Lambs: supposedly an ironic reference to the Pascal Lamb badge and the role of the regiment under one of its first colonels, the notorious Percy Kirke, in suppressing the West Country in the aftermath of the Monmouth Rebellion in 1685, though it seems to predate the latter in origin.

The Tangerines: from service at Tangier.

BADGE
The Pascal Lamb is known to have been worn by the regiment as early as 1685 and may have been adopted as a Christian emblem in its struggle against the Moors at Tangier. It is also said to have been granted by Catherine of Braganza, whose father, King John of Portugal, had a strong personal devotion to John the Baptist – but this is only speculation.

MOTTOES
Pristinae virtutis memor ('Mindful of our ancient valour').
Vel exuviae triumphans ('Even in defeat there can be triumph').

CUSTOMS
The regiment possessed a third Colour in its old green facing colour, commemorating its role as a marine force at the Glorious First of June in 1794. Despite additional Colours being discontinued in 1715, it was never fully withdrawn and was officially restored to the regiment in 1825. Third Colours were then banned by King William IV in 1835, but he permitted them to be retained though not paraded. In fact, the third Colour was paraded in 1927 and on the final parade of The Queen's Royal Surrey Regiment before amalgamation in 1992. The regimental quick march was originally 'The Old Queen's', partly based on the British national

anthem. In 1881, however, Queen Victoria queried whether there was any authority to use the national anthem for such a purpose. None was found and until the official approval of 'Braganza' in 1903, based on the old Portuguese national anthem, the regiment was known as 'The Silent Battalion' since it opted for no music until a new march was approved.

FACINGS
Royal blue.

REGIMENTAL MARCHES
'Braganza' (quick march).
'Scipio' (slow march).
'We'll gang nae mair to yon toun' (2nd Battalion).

COLOURS
Holy Trinity Church, Guildford; Guildford Cathedral; Regimental Museum.

MEMORIALS
Holy Trinity Church, Guildford; Guildford Cathedral; Putney Heath (Foundation of the Regiment); St George's Church, Napierville, Pietermaritzburg, and Clouston, Colenso, KwaZulu-Natal, and North Road, Kroonstad (all 2nd Battalion), South Africa.

BATTLE HONOURS
Tangiers 1662–80, Namur 1695, Vimiera, Corunna, Salamanca, Vittoria, Pyrenees, Nivelle, Toulouse, Peninsula, Ghuznee 1839, Khelat, Afghanistan 1839, South Africa 1851–3, Taku Forts, Pekin 1860, Burma 1885–7, Tirah, Relief of Ladysmith, South Africa 1899–1902.
Retreat from Mons, Ypres 1914 '17 '18, Somme 1916 '18, Messines 1917, Vittorio Veneto, Macedonia 1916–17, Gallipoli 1915, Palestine 1917–18, Mesopotamia 1915–18, North West Frontier India 1916–17, Afghanistan 1919.
Villers Bocage, Tobruk 1941, El Alamein, Medenine, Salerno, Monte Camino, Anzio, Gemmano Ridge, North Arakan, Kohima.

LATER LINEAGE
Amalgamated in 1959 with The East Surrey Regiment as The Queen's Royal Surrey Regiment. In 1966 this became 1st Battalion, The Queen's Regiment. A four-battalion regiment, The Queen's was reduced to three battalions in 1970. In turn, the Queen's Regiment amalgamated in 1992 with The Royal Hampshire Regiment as The Princess of Wales's Royal Regiment (Queen's and Royal Hampshires).

MUSEUMS
The Queen's Royal Surrey Regiment Museum, Clandon Park, Guildford, Surrey GU4 7RQ (telephone: 01483 223419; fax: 01483 224636; website: www.surrey-online.uk/queenssurreys). Additional items are displayed in *The Princess of Wales's Royal Regiment and Queen's Regiment Museum*, Dover Castle, Dover, Kent CT16 1HU (telephone: 01304 240121).

SUSSEX

The Royal Sussex Regiment
(35th and 107th Foot)

ORIGINS AND DEVELOPMENT

The 35th was raised in Belfast in 1701 as the Earl of Donegall's Regiment, being affiliated to Dorset in 1782 but renamed The Sussex Regiment in 1804. It received its Royal title in 1832. The 107th was raised at Chinsurah by the East India Company as the 3rd Bengal European Light Infantry in 1853, transferring to the British establishment in 1862. In 1881 the two were linked as The Royal Sussex Regiment. Reduced to a single battalion in 1948, it became the 3rd Battalion, The Queen's Regiment in 1966.

HISTORY

The 35th crossed the Atlantic four times during the eighteenth century, participating in the seizure of Louisburg in 1758 and being present at Quebec in 1759 and at Bunker Hill in 1775. It was Charles Lennox, Duke of Richmond, who persuaded the authorities to transfer the Sussex affiliation to the 35th from the 25th Foot (later The King's Own Scottish Borderers) in 1804. The Duke, who had joined the 35th in 1787, is perhaps best known, however, as the husband of the hostess at the famous ball in Brussels on the eve of Waterloo. In 1800 the 35th took part in the

The Royal Sussex at Abu Klea, earning its unique battle honour.

117

capture of Malta from the French, its King's Colour being the first raised over Valletta. Twenty soldiers from the 1st Battalion, wearing red serge coats borrowed from the Guards' Camel Regiment, were put into two boats towed by a steamer to make the last dash up the Nile towards Khartoum in January 1885 in a vain effort to save Charles Gordon, the expectation being that the sight of red coats on the river would be sufficient to throw the Mahdist forces into panic. In the event, the little force arrived at Khartoum two days too late and was forced to withdraw. The earlier battle against the Mahdists at Abu Klea, in which the British square was temporarily breached, resulted in a battle honour unique to the regiment. During the First World War the regiment furnished twenty-three battalions. It was known to the Germans as the 'Iron Regiment' and, interestingly, when surrendering to the regiment in Tripoli in 1943 General von Arnim also used this nickname.

VICTORIA CROSSES
Third Maori War (1); First World War (3); Second World War (1). Of these, two are in the Regimental Museum.

NICKNAMES
The Orange Lilies: from the original facings granted by King William III as a mark of favour to the 3rd Earl of Donegall, who had raised the regiment at his own expense; also a reference to the fleur-de-lys of the French Royal Roussillon Regiment, defeated by the 35th at Quebec.

The Haddocks: from the dolphins on the arms of Brighton.

BADGE
The 'Roussillon' Plume was awarded in 1879 in commemoration of beating the French Royal Roussillon Regiment at Quebec, the 35th taking the distinctive white plumes of the French regiment and putting them in their own caps. The remainder of the badge was that of the Order of the Garter with the Cross of St George on an eight-pointed Star. The 5th (Cinque Ports) Battalion has the Arms of the Cinque Ports as the central part of its badge.

MOTTO
Honi soit qui mal y pense ('Let him who thinks evil of it be ashamed').

FACINGS
Royal blue.

REGIMENTAL MARCHES
'Royal Sussex' (quick march, 1st Battalion).
'The Lass of Richmond Hill' (quick march, 2nd Battalion).
'Roussillon' (slow march).
'Sussex by the Sea' (marching song).

COLOURS
Chichester Cathedral; the Parish Churches of Hastings and Horsham.

MEMORIALS
West Pier, Brighton; Royal Pavilion, Brighton; Eastbourne Pier.

BATTLE HONOURS
Gibraltar 1704–5, Louisburg, Quebec 1759, Martinique 1762, Havannah, St

The memorial by Eastbourne Pier to men of The Royal Sussex Regiment lost in actions up to 1898.

Lucia 1778, Maida, Egypt 1882, Abu Klea, Nile 1884–5, South Africa 1900–02, Afghanistan 1919.

Retreat from Mons, Marne 1914 '18, Ypres 1914 '17 '18, Somme 1916 '18, Pilckem, Hindenburg Line, Italy 1917 '18, Gallipoli 1915, Palestine 1917–18, North West Frontier India 1915 '16-17.

North West Europe 1940, Abyssinia 1941, Omars, Alam el Halfa, El Alamein, Akarit, North Africa 1940–3, Cassino II, Italy 1944–5, Burma 1943–5.

LATER LINEAGE

A four-battalion regiment, The Queen's was reduced to three battalions in 1970. In turn, The Queen's Regiment amalgamated in 1992 with The Royal Hampshire Regiment as The Princess of Wales's Royal Regiment (Queen's and Royal Hampshires).

MUSEUM

The Royal Sussex Regiment Museum, Redoubt Fortress, Royal Parade, Eastbourne, East Sussex BN22 7AQ (telephone: 01323 410300; fax: 01323 439882; e-mail: redoubt@breathemail.net; website: www.eastbournemuseums.co.uk).

WARWICKSHIRE

The Royal Warwickshire Regiment
(6th Foot)

ORIGINS AND DEVELOPMENT

The 6th was raised by Sir Walter Vane in 1674 for the Dutch service. Taken into English service in 1688, it became affiliated to Warwickshire in 1782. It received its Royal title in 1832 and, in 1881, became The Royal Warwickshire Regiment. A 2nd Battalion existed from 1857 until 1948, when the 1st Battalion was disbanded and the 2nd redesignated as the 1st. In 1963, upon transfer to the Fusilier Brigade, it was renamed The Royal Warwickshire Fusiliers. In 1968 it joined The Royal Regiment of Fusiliers.

HISTORY

Crossing to England with William III's army, the 6th served in the Irish campaign, being present at the Boyne, before returning to Flanders for the siege of Namur in 1695. During the War of Spanish Succession the 6th was in Spain, where it was captured at Brihuega in December 1710. Placed on the Irish establishment after its exchange, the 6th did not return to the English establishment until 1739. It participated in the disastrous expedition to Cartagena in 1741–2, suffering heavy losses from yellow fever. Stationed in Scotland at the start of the Jacobite uprising, the 6th lost a number of small garrisons and two companies were annihilated at

An officer and private of The Royal Warwickshire Regiment in 1831, by Simkin.

120

In the Regimental Museum at Warwick is Terence Cuneo's painting of Montgomery signing the German surrender document at Luneberg Heath in May 1945.

Prestonpans. A drum of the 6th probably taken by the Jacobites at Prestonpans was found in a crofter's hut in 1905 and returned to the regiment. The 6th saw little further active service until returning to the West Indies to fight the Carib Indians on St Vincent in 1772, when it was so wasted by disease that it was sent home from New York rather than being employed against the American colonists in 1776. In Ireland in 1796, the regiment covered the retreat of various Irish auxiliaries from Castlebar in the face of an invading French force in August 1798. Service followed in Canada and the 6th then served through both the retreat to Corunna and the disastrous Walcheren expedition in 1809. The 6th particularly distinguished itself at Orthes in the Peninsula on 27th February 1814. Imperial garrison service took in South Africa, India and Aden before the 6th saw active service in the Eighth Kaffir (Cape Frontier) War (1850–3), the Hazara expedition on the North West Frontier in 1868 and the Sudan campaign of 1898. The newly formed 2nd Battalion saw service against insurgents in Jamaica in 1865 and in the South African War. Both Field Marshal Viscount Montgomery and Field Marshal Viscount Slim served with the regiment during the First World War, Montgomery being commissioned into the 1st Battalion in 1908 and Slim into the 9th (Service) Battalion in 1914. Montgomery won the Distinguished Service Order with the battalion in October 1914 before serving in a number of staff appointments on the Western Front. Slim served at Gallipoli and in Mesopotamia, winning the Military Cross in March 1917. He transferred to the Indian Army in 1919, subsequently serving with the Gurkhas. Of thirty-one battalions formed during the First World War, twenty served overseas. In the Second World War, the 2nd, 1/7th and 8th Battalions saw hard service during the retreat to Dunkirk in May 1940, the 2nd Battalion at Wormhoudt having some captured men massacred by German *Schutzstaffel* troops. The 2nd and 1/7th both fought in Normandy in June 1944.

The 1st Battalion served mostly on the North West Frontier before seeing some action in Burma against the Japanese in April 1945. The 8th Battalion was mobilised in October 1945 for service in the Middle East until 1947, when it became the nucleus for a new unit, the 18th Battalion Parachute Battalion. In 1948 the 1st Battalion returned from internal security duties in Palestine and was stationed in Warwick until January 1951, when it went to Graz, Austria. In 1953 the battalion joined the Commonwealth Division in Korea, despite the armistice being signed, and returned home in 1955 via Cyprus, carrying out internal security duties against EOKA. Between 1956 and 1963 the battalion served in Ireland, Aden, Hong Kong and the British Army of the Rhine. In 1960 the regiment joined the Forester Brigade, but after changes in the army in 1963 it left the Forester Brigade and joined the Fusilier Brigade along with The Royal Northumberland Fusiliers, The Royal Fusiliers and The Lancashire Fusiliers. This became the Royal Regiment of Fusiliers in 1968.

VICTORIA CROSSES
First World War (6). Of these, four are in the Regimental Museum.

NICKNAMES
The Dutch Guards: from the lingering Dutch influence in the regiment and the number of officers familiar with the Dutch language.
Guise's Greens: from the green facings and John Guise, their colonel between 1738 and 1765.
The Saucy Sixth: from the regimental number.
The Warwickshire Lads: from the popular song 'Warwickshire Lads and Lasses', composed by Charles Dibdin in 1769 with words by David Garrick for Shakespeare celebrations at Stratford-upon-Avon. It became the regimental march in 1782.

BADGE
The White Antelope with Gold Collar and Chain was said to have originated from a standard of a Spanish regiment captured at Saragossa in 1710. Alternatively, it may have been derived from a badge of the Lancastrian kings.

MOTTO
Honi soit qui mal y pense ('Let him who thinks evil of it be ashamed').

CUSTOMS
An antelope was adopted as a regimental mascot in 1877 and an antelope continues to be the mascot of The Royal Regiment of Fusiliers. The collar badge was the Bear and Ragged Staff associated with the Earls of Warwick.

FACINGS
Royal blue.

REGIMENTAL MARCHES
'The Warwickshire Lads' (quick march).
'McBean's March' (slow march).

COLOURS
St Mary's Church, Warwick; Coventry Cathedral; Regimental Museum.

MEMORIALS
Bloemfontein, South Africa (2nd Battalion); Nuneaton; Birmingham; Warwick.

BATTLE HONOURS
Namur 1695, Martinique 1794, Rolica, Vimiero, Corunna, Vittoria, Pyrenees, Nivelle, Orthes, Peninsula, Niagara, South Africa 1846–7, 1851–2–3, Atbara, Khartoum, South Africa 1899–1902.

Le Cateau, Ypres 1914 '15 '17, Namur 1914, Somme 1914–15, Arras 1917–18, Hindenburg Line, Lys, Piave, Sari Bair, Baghdad.

Ypres-Comines Canal, Defence of Escaut, Wormhoudt, Normandy Landing, Mont Pincon, Caen, Venraij, Bremen, North West Europe 1940 '44–5, Burma 1945.

LATER LINEAGE
A four-battalion regiment when created, The Royal Regiment of Fusiliers was reduced to three battalions in 1969 and to two battalions in 1992.

MUSEUMS
The Royal Regiment of Fusiliers (Royal Warwickshire) Museum, St John's House, Warwick CV34 4NF (telephone: 01926 491653; fax: 01869 257633; website: www.army.mod.uk/fusiliers).

WESTMORLAND
(see **Cumberland**)

WILTSHIRE

The Wiltshire Regiment (Duke of Edinburgh's)
(62nd and 99th Foot)

ORIGINS AND DEVELOPMENT

The 62nd was raised in Exeter from the 2/4th Foot in 1756 and affiliated to Wiltshire in 1782, while the 99th or Lanarkshire Regiment was raised in Glasgow in 1824 and became The Duke of Edinburgh's in 1874. In 1881 the two regiments were linked as the 1st and 2nd Battalions, The Duke of Edinburgh's Wiltshire Regiment. This was changed to The Wiltshire Regiment (Duke of Edinburgh's) in 1920. Reduced to a single battalion in 1948. Amalgamated 1959.

HISTORY

The 62nd initially saw much service as a marine force, earning its battle honour of Louisburg in 1758 while under Admiral Boscawen, this great French fortress on Cape Breton island guarding the mouth of the St Lawrence river and, thus, the route to Quebec. The 62nd was also present at the capture of Quebec itself in September 1759. Sent to Ireland, a detachment of the 62nd held the castle of Carrickfergus against a superior force landed from a French raiding expedition on 21st February 1760 until their ammunition was exhausted. The Carrickfergus Cup was presented to Lieutenant Benjamin Hall by the Mayor and Corporation of Carrickfergus for his gallantry during the French raid. After service against the Maroons on Jamaica, the 62nd was heavily involved in the American War of Independence, acting as light infantry. Forced to surrender with Burgoyne's army at Saratoga on 17th October 1777, the officers of the 62nd tore the Colours from

The 62nd Foot at the battle of Ferozeshah, India, 1845.

their pikes to prevent them falling into rebel hands. One was restored to the regiment in 1927. During the French Revolutionary and Napoleonic Wars the 1/62nd was once more in the West Indies fighting Maroons, then in Egypt and Italy, before being despatched to Canada during the Anglo-American War (1812–14). During the First Sikh War, the 62nd was at the two-day battle of Ferozeshah on 21st–22nd December 1845. Tasked to advance in the open and without support, the regiment pressed its attack despite the loss of most of its officers and heavy casualties. In all, the 62nd spent seventeen years in India, subsequently also seeing service in the Crimea. The 99th was initially raised for service at Mauritius and saw action in the First Maori War, attacking the Ohaeawai pa of the Maori leader, Honi Heke, in June 1845. Subsequently, stationed at Aldershot and often required to find a guard for the Royal Pavilion, its good drill and turnout is supposedly the origin of the phase 'dressed up to the Nines'. During the First World War, seven battalions of the regiment served overseas, seeing action in all theatres with the 5th Battalion experiencing particularly hard service in Mesopotamia. In the Second World War, the 2nd Battalion campaigned in Sicily and in Italy, including service in the Anzio bridgehead in 1943. The 1st Battalion saw action against the Japanese in the Arakan in February 1944, while the 4th and 5th battalions served in the celebrated 43rd (Wessex) Division from Normandy to the Rhine. Post-war tours included one of Cyprus from 1956 to 1958, in which the battalion succeeded in trapping and killing EOKA's second-in-command, Matsis.

VICTORIA CROSSES
First World War (1); Second World War (1). Both are displayed in the Regimental Museum.

NICKNAMES
The Springers: from the light infantry command 'Spring up' (advance) during the American War of Independence.
The Moon Rakers: from the old story that Wiltshire peasants tried to rake the moon from a pond when mistaking its reflection for a cheese.
The Splashers: from the regiment's buttons, which had a dent, commemorating the 62nd's defence of Carrickfergus Castle. Having run out of ammunition, the men hurled bricks and stones but also fired off their buttons.

BADGE
The Ducal Coronet and Cipher derive from the 99th as the Duke of Edinburgh's, while the Cross Patee, based on the Maltese Cross, was that of the 62nd.

MOTTO
Honi soit qui mal y pense ('Let him who thinks evil of it be ashamed').

CUSTOMS
In memory of Ferozeshah, when the non-commissioned officers brought the regiment and Colours out of action, the Colours were handed to the custody of the sergeants' mess thereafter on the annual anniversary of the battle. 'Rule Britannia' would be played before the regiment's own march in band programmes to commemorate marine service in the eighteenth century.

FACINGS
Salmon buff.

REGIMENTAL MARCHES
'The Wiltshires' (based on the old Wiltshire song 'The Vly be on the Turmut').

COLOURS
St James's Church, Devizes; Salisbury Cathedral; St Giles's Church, Edinburgh (99th).

MEMORIALS
St James's Church, Devizes (Zulu War).

BATTLE HONOURS
Louisburg, Nive, Peninsula, New Zealand, Ferozeshah, Sobraon, Sevastopol, Pekin 1860, South Africa 1879, 1900–02.
Mons, Messines 1914 '17, Ypres 1914 '17, Somme 1916 '18, Arras 1917, Bapaume 1918, Macedonia 1915–18, Gallipoli 1915–16, Palestine 1917–18, Baghdad.
Defence of Arras, Hill 112, Maltot, Mont Pincon, Seine 1944, Cleve, Gargliano Crossing, Anzio, Rome, North Arakan.

LATER LINEAGE
Amalgamated in 1959 with The Royal Berkshire Regiment (Princess Charlotte of Wales's) as The Duke of Edinburgh's Royal Regiment (Berkshire and Wiltshire). In 1994 there was a further amalgamation with The Gloucestershire Regiment as The Royal Gloucestershire, Berkshire and Wiltshire Regiment.

MUSEUMS
The Royal Gloucestershire, Berkshire and Wiltshire Regiment (Salisbury) Museum, The Wardrobe, 58 The Close, Salisbury, Wiltshire SP1 2EX (telephone: 01722 414536; fax: 01722 421626; website: www.thewardrobe.org.uk).

Colour Sergeant Harrill (Drum Major) of 1st Battalion, The Duke of Edinburgh's Royal Regiment.

WORCESTERSHIRE

The Worcestershire Regiment
(29th and 36th Foot)

ORIGINS AND DEVELOPMENT

The 29th Foot was raised in 1694 as Farrington's Regiment, while the 36th was raised in 1701 as Charlemont's Regiment. In 1782, the 29th was affiliated to Worcestershire and the 36th to Herefordshire. In 1881 they were linked as the 1st and 2nd Battalions, The Worcestershire Regiment. Reduced to a single battalion in 1948. Amalgamated 1970.

HISTORY

Farrington's Regiment was disbanded in 1698 following the end of the Nine Years War but then raised again with the same officers in March 1702 and sent to Ireland. The 36th, meanwhile, which had been raised in Ireland, was despatched on an unsuccessful expedition to capture Cadiz before going on to Guadaloupe in the West Indies in 1703 and returning to the Spanish theatre in the War of Spanish Succession. Later serving in North America, it was a detachment of the 29th that became involved in the 'Boston Massacre' on 5th March 1770, a small group opening fire on a mob and killing four people. Captain Preston and eight men were tried, with Preston and six men being acquitted and the other two being branded and discharged from the army. The 36th went to India in 1783, campaigning against Tippoo Sahib of Mysore and being present at the storming of Bangalore on 18th October 1791. In Europe, meanwhile, the 29th won a naval crown for its service as marines at the naval battle of the Glorious First of June in 1794, another lingering echo being the adoption of 'Hearts of Oak' as one of the regimental marches. It went on to serve in the Peninsular War, distinguishing itself at Rolica on 15th August 1808. Rolica was the last battle at which the army as a whole wore queues

The 29th Foot at the Battle of Vimiero, 1808.

At Gheluvelt on 31st October 1914 the 2nd Battalion of the Worcesters held the German advance.

and powdered hair, but it is said that the men of the 29th were the last to cut their hair and still fought at Vimiero on 21st August in the old style. The 36th also fought through the Peninsular Campaign and after Vimiero was praised by Wellington as 'an example to the army'. One of the most memorable incidents in the regiment's history was the counter-attack carried out by the 2nd Battalion at a critical moment at Gheluvelt near Ypres on 31st October 1914. With the Germans close to breaking through the British line, the Worcesters represented the only uncommitted reserve when they successfully halted the German advance. The 4th Battalion took part in the landing at V Beach at Cape Helles, Gallipoli, on 25th April 1915, while the 11th Battalion served in Macedonia, taking the Bulgarian position known as the Scabbard on 24th April 1917, though it was subsequently forced to withdraw. In the Second World War the 7th and 8th Battalions suffered heavily in the retreat to Dunkirk, the 2nd and 7th Battalions served in Burma and the 1st Battalion saw service in Italian East Africa and North Africa, most of the men being captured at Tobruk in June 1942. On being re-formed, the 1st Battalion landed in Normandy and served in North West Europe. After the war, the regiment saw service in Malaya.

VICTORIA CROSSES
    First World War (9). Of these, six are in the Regimental Museum.

NICKNAMES
    The Ever-Sworded: from the custom of officers of the 29th wearing swords in the mess following a surprise attack by North American Indians in 1746. The order for all to wear swords was finally rescinded in 1842, after which swords were worn only by the Captain of the Week and the orderly officer.
    The Vein Openers: from supposedly being the regiment that shed the first blood in the Boston Massacre, which led to the American War of Independence.
    The Star of the Line (29th): from the Star badge, as described below.
    The Saucy Greens (36th): from the regimental number and alleged prowess with

young ladies.

The Firms: from the motto (see below).

BADGE

A silver oval Star mounted with a gilt oval Garter, enclosing a silver lion on a label inscribed with the motto 'Firm' (which was that of the 36th).

MOTTO

Firm.

CUSTOMS

A larger version of the regimental Star badge was borne on the black ammunition wallets in the eighteenth century but when the old cross-belt equipment was discontinued in 1784 the regiment received permission to wear their Stars on their issue packs, even in khaki field service. The Worcesters and The Royal Lincolnshire Regiment played each other's regimental marches before their own on ceremonial occasions to mark their service together at Sobraon in February 1846.

FACINGS

White.

REGIMENTAL MARCHES

'Hearts of Oak' (assembly march).

'Royal Windsor' (quick march).

'Duchess of Kent' (slow march).

COLOURS

Worcester Cathedral; Norton Church.

MEMORIALS

Worcester Cathedral; Pershore Abbey; Memorial House, Herentage, Gheluvelt, Ypres, Belgium (2nd Battalion); President Avenue, Bloemfontein, Orange Free State, and Memorial Hill, Singersfontein, Colesberg, South Africa (both 2nd Battalion).

BATTLE HONOURS

Ramillies, Mysore, Hindoostan, Rolica, Vimiero, Corunna, Talavera, Albuhera, Salamanca, Pyrenees, Nivelle, Nive, Orthes, Toulouse, Peninsula, Ferozeshah, Sobraon, Chillianwallah, Goojerat, Punjaub, South Africa 1900–02.

Mons, Ypres 1914 '15 '17 '18, Gheluvelt, Neuve Chapelle, Somme 1916 '18, Cambrai, Lys, Italy 1917–18, Gallipoli 1915–16, Baghdad.

Mont Pincon, Seine 1944, Geilenkirchen, Goch, North West Europe 1940 '44–5, Keren, Gazala, Kohima, Mandalay, Burma 1944–5.

LATER LINEAGE

Amalgamated 1970 with The Sherwood Foresters (Nottinghamshire and Derbyshire Regiment) as The Worcestershire and Sherwood Foresters Regiment (29th/45th Foot).

MUSEUMS

Museum of the Worcestershire Regiment, Worcester City Museum and Art Gallery, Foregate Street, Worcester WR1 1DT (telephone: 01905 25371).

YORKSHIRE

The Duke of Wellington's Regiment (West Riding)
(33rd and 76th Foot)

ORIGINS AND DEVELOPMENT

The 33rd Foot was raised in Gloucester in 1702 as Huntingdon's Regiment, the West Riding in 1782. The 76th was raised in 1787. In 1853, the year after the death of the Duke of Wellington, who had commanded the 33rd, Queen Victoria granted the secondary title of The Duke of Wellington's. The two were linked as the 1st and 2nd Battalion, The Duke of Wellington's (West Riding Regiment) in 1881, becoming The Duke of Wellington's Regiment (West Riding) in 1921. Reduced to a single battalion in 1948.

HISTORY

The 33rd served in the Peninsula during the War of Spanish Succession, being forced to surrender both after Almanza on 25th April 1709 and at Brigheuga in December 1710. The 33rd was also at Dettingen on 27th June 1743 and at Fontenoy on 11th May 1745. The regiment saw considerable service in the American War of Independence, fighting at Brandywine and Germantown in 1777 and in the southern campaigns in the Carolinas in 1780–1, being part of Cornwallis's army that surrendered at Yorktown in October 1781. Arthur Wellesley, first Duke of Wellington, was a subaltern in the 76th in 1787 when the regiment was first raised and later held a major's commission in the 33rd, commanding the regiment in Flanders in 1794–5 and becoming colonel in 1806. The 76th was specifically raised for service in India and proceeded there in 1788, remaining for almost twenty years. While Wellesley himself commanded the British campaign in the Deccan during the

A private of the 33rd Foot during the American War of Independence.

130

Second Maratha War, the 76th served further north under Gerald Lake, distinguishing itself in the assault on Ally Ghur on 4th September 1803 and the subsequent battles at Delhi on 16th September and Laswaree on 1st November. Returning to England in 1806, the 76th saw service in the Corunna campaign in 1809 and in the closing stages of Wellington's victories in the Peninsula, notably at Nive in December 1813. Service followed for the 76th in Canada and Ireland. The 33rd meanwhile played a significant role in the repulse of Napoleon's Imperial Guard at Waterloo on 18th June 1815. Subsequently, the 33rd participated in the Crimean War, the Indian Mutiny and the Abyssinian expedition in 1867–8, the explorer and newspaper correspondent H. M. Stanley characterising it in the latter as an 'Irish regiment' through the large number of Irishmen in the ranks. At Paardeburg on 19th February 1900 the 2nd Battalion went straight into a frontal assault on the Boer positions from a long march and without having eaten for twenty-four hours. The battalion again lost heavily at Hill 60 on the Western Front in April 1915. In the Second World War the 2nd Battalion took part in the longest retreat in British military history, from Rangoon to Imphal in Assam between February and May 1942 as part of the 17th Indian Division. The 1st Battalion saw heavy fighting at Anzio in January 1944. In the Korean War, the regiment held the feature known as 'The Hook' against repeated mass Chinese attacks in May 1953.

Victoria Crosses
Abyssinia, 1868 (2); South African War (1); First World War (5); Second World War (1). Of these, four are in the Regimental Museum.

Nicknames
The Havercake Lads (33rd): from the supposed method of recruiting sergeants carrying oatcakes on their swords as a means of attracting men.
The Immortals: from the high losses suffered in India.
The Duke's: from the title.
The Old Seven and Sixpennies (76th): from the regimental number.

Badge
The badge consists of the Arms of the Duke of Wellington, but with the Red Demi-lion supporting a pennon bearing the Cross of St George, which represents that given to the sovereign annually on the anniversary of Waterloo as the quit-rent (a rent paid by a freeholder as a token of service) for the Stratfield Saye estate in Hampshire granted the Duke for his victory at Waterloo. A similar custom is maintained with respect to the Duke of Marlborough's estate at Blenheim near Woodstock in Oxfordshire.

Motto
Virtutis fortuna comes ('Success abides with valour'). (It is sometimes rendered as 'Fortune favours the brave' but this would more properly be *Audaces fortuna juvat*.)

Customs
The regiment's collar badge was a small elephant with a howdah, commemorating the years spent in India by the 76th. The 76th had also been presented with an additional pair of Colours while in India by the East India Company for its assault on the fortress of Ally Ghur and the subsequent advance on Delhi. In 1835 King William IV directed that no additional Colours should be borne by any regiment, but The Duke of Wellington's alone was permitted to carry the Honorary Colours on

parade. The Honorary Colours bore five Indian battle honours and four from the Peninsular War, since the 76th carried them there in battle. Regimental musical customs included playing 'Cock o' the North' during the Beating the Retreat ceremony in honour of Lieutenant Colonel Lloyd, killed with the 1st Battalion in South Africa, and 'Honours of War' during the ceremony of Bearing Tattoo to commemorate Waterloo.

FACINGS
Scarlet.

REGIMENTAL MARCHES
'On Ilkley Moor B'at T'at'.
'I'm Ninety Five'.
'Scotland the Brave'.
'The Wellesley'.

COLOURS
York Minster; Halifax Parish Church.

MEMORIALS
York Minster; Halifax Parish Church; President Avenue, Bloemfontein, Orange Free State (1st and 2nd Battalions); Vendusie Drift, Paardeburg, Orange Free State, Petronella, and Diamond Hill, South Africa (all 1st Battalion).

BATTLE HONOURS
Dettingen, Mysore, Seringapatam, Ally Ghur, Delhi 1803, Leswarree, Deig, Corunna, Nive, Peninsula, Waterloo, Alma, Inkerman, Sevastopol, Abyssinia, Relief of Kimberley, Paardeburg, South Africa 1900–02, Afghanistan 1919.
Mons, Marne 1914 '18, Ypres 1914 '18, Hill 60, Somme 1916 '18, Arras 1917 '18, Cambrai 1917 '18, Lys, Piave 1918, Landing at Suvla.
Dunkirk, St Valery-en-Caux, Fontenay le Pesnil, North West Europe 1940 '44–5, Djebel bou Aoukaz 1943, Anzio, Monte Ceco, Sittang 1942, Chindits 1944, Burma 1942–4, The Hook 1953, Korea 1952–3.

LATER LINEAGE
The regiment has remained unscathed amid post-1945 reductions and amalgamations.

MUSEUMS
The Duke of Wellington's Regimental Museum, Bankfield Museum, Akroyd Park, Boothtown Road, Halifax, West Yorkshire HX3 6HG (telephone: 01422 354823; website: www.army.mod.uk/ceremonialandheritage/museums).

The East Yorkshire Regiment (The Duke of York's Own) (15th Foot)

ORIGINS AND DEVELOPMENT
The 15th was raised in June 1685 as Clifton's Regiment, becoming affiliated to the East Riding of Yorkshire in 1782. In 1881 it became The East Yorkshire Regiment (The Duke of York's Own). A 2nd Battalion existed from 1858 to 1948. Amalgamated 1958.

A mounted infantryman of The East Yorkshire Regiment, 1901, from a painting by Lovett.

HISTORY

The early service of the 15th was in Scotland, where the regiment took Lethinly Castle in May 1690, and Flanders, where it was captured at Dixmude in July 1695. The regiment played a prominent part in Marlborough's victories and, in 1719, helped repel a Spanish raid on Scotland. It suffered grievously from disease in the West Indies in 1741 at Cartagena, Cuba and Porto Bello. Serving in Flanders, it was recalled to help suppress the second Jacobite rising in 1745–6. In the Seven Years War it served in North America, being present at the fall of Louisburg in 1758 and at Quebec in 1759. Ten officers of the regiment subsequently acted as provincial governors in North America. There was further service in North America during the War of Independence, with spells in the West Indies both before and after the war, detachments of the regiment being captured at St Eustatius and on St Kitts in 1779. Still in the West Indies during the French Revolutionary War, on Dominica in 1795–6 the 15th lost to disease all but seven of the 102 wives accompanying the regiment. The 1/15th saw little active service for over sixty years after the capture of Guadaloupe in 1810, where 276 men fell victim to disease in eighteen months, beyond a riot in Montreal in May 1832. The 2/15th, however, took part in the Second Afghan War as part of Sir Robert Phayre's relief force, just beaten to Kandahar in August 1880 by that of Sir Frederick Roberts. At Ypres in April 1915 the 2nd Battalion helped restore the line after the first use of gas by the Germans on the Western Front. In the Second World War the regiment was the only one to have two battalions (the 2nd and 5th) involved in the initial assault landings in Normandy on 6th June 1944. The 4th Battalion was almost entirely destroyed at

133

The Battle Flag of the 2nd Battalion, The East Yorkshire Regiment, being carried ashore on the Normandy beaches during D-Day, 6th June 1944.

Gazala in the Western Desert in May and June 1942, while the 1st Battalion served in Burma in the final advance on Rangoon in April 1945.

VICTORIA CROSSES
First World War (4); Second World War (1). Of these, four are in the Regimental Museum.

NICKNAMES
The Snappers: from the 15th running out of ammunition at Brandywine on 11th September 1777 during the American War of Independence and confusing the enemy by snapping the locks on their powder charges to maintain the appearance of firing.

BADGE
The White Rose of York in a laurel wreath on an eight-pointed Star.

MOTTO
Honi soit qui mal y pense ('Let him who thinks evil of it be ashamed').

CUSTOMS
In memory of James Wolfe, under whom the regiment served at Louisburg and Quebec, officers wore a black line in the gold lace of their full dress and, subsequently, a black background to the silver rose worn on the collar. On the anniversary of Quebec (13th September) itself, bunches of white roses (for Yorkshire) were carried on the pikes of the Colours. Wolfe is still recalled in the regiment's modern lineal descendant in the black background to the silver rose worn in the collar badge. It was also the custom for a young officer detailed to carry a Colour for the first time to invite the Colour party and escort to drink a glass of champagne with him after the parade.

FACINGS
White.

REGIMENTAL MARCHES
'The Yorkshire Lass' (quick march).
'The 15th von England' (slow march).

COLOURS
Beverley Minster; Holy Trinity Church, Hull.

MEMORIALS
Londesborough Barracks, Hull; Beverley Minster.

BATTLE HONOURS
Blenheim, Ramillies, Oudenarde, Malplaquet, Louisburg, Quebec 1759, Martinique 1762, Havannah, St Lucia 1778, Martinique 1794, 1809, Guadaloupe 1810, Afghanistan 1879–80, South Africa 1900–02.
Aisne 1914 '18, Armentières 1914, Ypres 1915 '17 '18, Arras 1917 '18, Loos, Somme 1916, '18, Cambrai 1917 '18, Selle, Doiran 1917, Gallipoli 1915.
Dunkirk 1940, Normandy Landing, Odon, Schaddenhof, North West Europe 1940 '44–5, Gazala, El Alamein, Mareth, Sicily 1943, Burma 1942–5.

LATER LINEAGE
Amalgamated in 1958 with The West Yorkshire Regiment (The Prince of Wales's Own) as The Prince of Wales's Own Regiment of Yorkshire.

MUSEUMS
The Prince of Wales's Own Regiment of Yorkshire Regimental Museum, 3 Tower Street, York YO1 9SB (telephone: 01904 662790; fax: 01904 658824).

The Green Howards
(Alexandra, Princess of Wales's Own Yorkshire Regiment)
(19th Foot)

ORIGINS AND DEVELOPMENT
The 19th was raised by Francis Luttrell of Dunster Castle, Somerset, in 1688. It was affiliated to the North Riding in 1782. It became Princess Alexandra's in 1875 when she presented new Colours to the 1st Battalion. In 1881 it became The Princess of Wales's Own (Yorkshire Regiment) and, in 1902, Alexandra, Princess of Wales's Own (Yorkshire Regiment). The title, which began as the regiment's nickname as indicated below, was only adopted in 1921 when it became The Green Howards (Alexandra, Princess of Wales's Own Yorkshire Regiment). A 2nd Battalion existed in the periods 1689–98, 1756–8, 1858–1949 and 1952–6.

HISTORY
The 19th was a double-battalion regiment from 1689 to 1698, the 2/19th seeing active service for the first time at the Boyne in Ireland on 1st July 1690 (later celebrated on 12th July) and a combined force from both battalions being present at Landen in Flanders in 1693, one of the bloodiest battles of the horse and musket period. One rarity is an original musket issued on the regiment's formation, together with an equally rare cartridge bandoleer – twelve wooden bottles holding the

Lieutenant General the Honourable Sir Charles Howard KB, who gave his name to the regiment. He was the second son of the third Earl of Carlisle, who built Castle Howard in North Yorkshire.

powder charge and known to contemporaries as 'The Twelve Apostles'. The 19th returned to Flanders for Marlborough's campaigns, winning its first battle honour at great cost at Malplaquet on 11th September 1709 and serving at the sieges of Douai and Bouchain. The regiment was in Flanders for a third time during the War of Austrian Succession, its nickname being associated with Fontenoy in 1745. The 19th served in Ceylon for most of the period between 1796 and 1820, with occasional forays to India as in the operations against Tippoo Sahib of Mysore in 1799. Consequently, it missed the Napoleonic Wars in Europe completely, but soldiered through the First, Second and Third Kandyan Wars. Indeed, many men of the regiment were killed in a massacre of prisoners after the capture of Kandy by rebels in June 1803 and, when the regiment finally left Ceylon in 1820, only two of those who had landed with it remained. At the Alma on 20th September 1854 the regiment stormed the Russian Great Redoubt, capturing seven Russian drums of the Minsk, Vladimir and Borodino regiments. At the assault on the Redan at Sevastopol in September 1855, Lieutenant Massy became a national hero as one of the first men into the fortification even though severely wounded. In 1868 the 1st Battalion campaigned against the Black Mountain tribes of the North West Frontier as well as taking part at Ginnis in the Sudan on 30th December 1885, when red coats were worn for the last time in battle. During the First World War the regiment raised twenty-four battalions and won twelve Victoria Crosses, the 2nd Battalion holding the Menin crossroads for sixteen days during the First Battle of Ypres in October and November 1914, suffering 683 casualties. The 4th and 5th Battalions were at the Second Battle of Ypres in April 1915 and the 6th Battalion at Gallipoli, taking the Lala Baba feature at Suvla Bay on 6th August 1915. Twelve battalions were raised in the Second World War and three Victoria Crosses won. The 1st Battalion was in Norway in April 1940, covering the retreat of the 15th Infantry Brigade from Kvam to Aandalsnes, where it was evacuated by the Royal Navy. The regiment served in Malaya from 1949 to 1952, the reconstituted 2nd Battalion serving in Suez and on Cyprus before once more being placed in 'suspended animation'. The regiment has since distinguished itself in Northern Ireland with fourteen tours between 1970 and 2002. A small contingent also served as medical assistants in Saudi Arabia during

A painting by Fortunio Matania of the 2nd Battalion, The Yorkshire Regiment (Green Howards) holding the Menin Crossroads, south-east of Ypres, in October 1914. The soldier in the foreground, Private Henry Tandey, was subsequently awarded the VC, DCM, MM and five mentions in despatches and survived the war.

the Gulf War in 1991. The 1st Battalion served in Bosnia from 1996 to 1997 and in Kosovo in 1999.

VICTORIA CROSSES

Crimean War (2); South African War (1); First World War (12); Second World War (3). Of these, sixteen are in the Regimental Museum.

NICKNAMES

The regiment's title began as its nickname in the 1744–5 campaign in Flanders when there were two regiments commanded by a Howard in the same brigade, the 3rd Foot wearing buff facings (The Buff Howards) and the 19th green facings.

BADGE

The badge surmounted by a Coronet is the initial letter of Princess Alexandra entwined with the Dannebrog or Danish Cross, Princess (later Queen) Alexandra being of the Danish royal family. As indicated above, 1875 was the year of her association with the regiment.

COLONELS-IN-CHIEF

The first Colonel-in-Chief was Queen Alexandra, who gave her name to the regiment and designed the badge. Her daughter, Maude, married the first king of Norway, Haakon VII, who became Colonel-in-Chief in 1942. On his death his son, King Olav V, followed him and today his son, King Harald V, is the present Colonel-in-Chief.

CUSTOMS

The annual 'Drummer Boy Walk' commemorates the supposed loss of a young drummer of the 19th in a tunnel in Richmond during the Napoleonic Wars when the sound of his drum could reputedly be heard for some time afterwards. Alma Day (20th September) is celebrated annually, five of the drums captured by the 19th being paraded by the 1st Battalion on this day.

FACINGS

Green, but not until 1901 after a twenty-year battle with the War Office, which had imposed white facings at the time of territorialisation in 1881.

REGIMENTAL MARCHES

'The Bonnie English Rose' (quick march).
'Marie Theresa' (slow march).

COLOURS

St Mary's Church, Richmond; County Hall, Northallerton; Town Hall, Middlesbrough; Regimental Museum. The 2nd Battalion Colours are hung in the Normandy Room of the Green Howards Museum, Richmond.

MEMORIALS

St Mary's Church, Richmond; British Cemetery, Fricourt, Somme, France (7th Battalion); York (South African War); Monument Farm, Vendusie Drift and Gruisbank, Paardeburg, Orange Free State, South Africa (1st Battalion); Crepon, Normandy (6th and 7th Battalions).

BATTLE HONOURS

Malplaquet, Belle Isle, Alma, Inkerman, Sevastopol, Tirah, Relief of Kimberley, Paardeburg, South Africa 1899–1902.
Ypres 1914 '15 '17, Loos, Somme 1916 '18, Arras 1917 '18, Messines 1917 '18, Valenciennes, Sambre, France and Flanders 1914–18, Vittorio Veneto, Suvla.
Norway 1940, Normandy Landing, North West Europe 1940 '44–5, Gazala, El Alamein, Mareth, Akarit, Sicily 1943, Minturno, Anzio.

LATER LINEAGE

The regiment has remained unscathed amid post-1881 and 1945 reductions and

A 'Warrior' armoured personnel carrier of 'A' (King Harald V) Company, 1st Battalion The Green Howards, operating as part of the large NATO force driving their armoured vehicles from Macedonia into Kosovo in June 1999.

amalgamations. It is the oldest of only two English line regiments not to be amalgamated; the other is the 22nd Foot (Cheshire Regiment).

MUSEUMS
The Green Howards Regimental Museum, Trinity Church Square, Richmond, North Yorkshire DL10 4QN (telephone: 01748 822133; fax: 01748 821924).

The King's Own Yorkshire Light Infantry (KOYLI)
(51st and 105th Foot)

ORIGINS AND DEVELOPMENT
The 51st Foot was raised in 1755 and affiliated to the West Riding in 1782. It was converted to a light infantry role in 1809 and designated The King's Own Light Infantry in 1821. The 105th was the 2nd Madras (European Light Infantry) Regiment, raised by the East India Company in 1839 and transferred to British service in 1861. The two were linked as The King's Own Yorkshire Light Infantry (South Yorkshire Regiment) in 1881, becoming The King's Own (Yorkshire Light Infantry) in 1897 and The King's Own Yorkshire Light Infantry in 1948, at which time the two regular battalions were amalgamated. In 1969 it became the 2nd Battalion, The Light Infantry.

HISTORY
The 51st was one of the Minden regiments, this being its first battle honour, earned on 1st August 1759. Sir John Moore, the effective creator of the British light infantry arm, was commissioned into the 51st in 1777, later being appointed its commanding officer in 1790 before receiving a brigade command. It was appropriate, therefore, that Moore's old regiment should be one of those converted to light infantry, albeit in tribute to him after his death at Corunna. As it happened, the 51st had been at Corunna and returned to the Peninsula in its new guise. At Badajoz on 6th April 1811 Ensign Joseph Dyas twice led the storming party into the breach of San Christobal Fort. Offered immediate promotion by Wellington into another regiment, Dyas declined to leave the 51st. At Waterloo the 51st was on the extreme right of the British line. In the Second Burma War (1852) it gained the battle honour of 'Pegu' and was later on the North West Frontier during the Second Afghan War. The 1st Battalion of the new linked regiment saw service in Burma

The Colours of the 51st Foot that were carried at the Battle of Waterloo, 1815.

139

again in 1885 and on the frontier in the Tirah campaign in 1897. Meanwhile, the 2nd Battalion had formed part of the Zhob Valley Field Force in 1890 and went on to distinguish itself in the South African War. In the First World War the 2nd Battalion was at Le Cateau on 26th August 1914, taking some six hundred casualties. The 1st Battalion reached France from Singapore in 1915 and was later to serve at Salonika before returning to the Western Front in 1918. In the Second World War both the 5th and 8th Battalions were converted to light anti-aircraft regiments and the 7th Battalion to armour. The 2nd Battalion took part in the longest retreat in British military history, that from Burma back to Assam on the frontier of India in the face of the Japanese in early 1942. After the war, the 1st Battalion served during the emergencies in Kenya, Aden and Cyprus and in Sarawak and Brunei during the Malaysian/Indonesian Confrontation.

VICTORIA CROSSES
South African War (1); First World War (7). Of these, four are in the Regimental Museum.

NICKNAMES
The Koylis: from the initials of 'King's Own Yorkshire Light Infantry'.

BADGE
A French Horn with the White Rose of York.

MOTTO
Cede nullis ('Yield to none').

CUSTOMS
Following the Loyal Toast, the second toast in the mess was to 'Ensign Dyas and the Stormers' in tribute to Dyas's gallantry at Badajoz. As a Minden regiment, white roses were worn on Minden Day.

FACINGS
Royal blue.

REGIMENTAL MARCHES
'Jockey to the Fair'.
'Minden March' (slow march).

COLOURS
The Regimental Museum.

MEMORIALS
York Minster; Modder River, South Africa (2nd Battalion).

BATTLE HONOURS
Minden, Corunna, Fuentes d'Onoro, Salamanca, Vittoria, Pyrenees, Nivelle, Orthes, Peninsula, Waterloo, Pegu, Ali Masjid, Afghanistan 1878–80, Burma 1885–7, Modder River, South Africa 1899–1902.

Mons, Le Cateau, Marne 1914, Messines 1914 '15 '17, Ypres 1914 '15 '17, Somme 1916 '18, Cambrai, Havrincourt, Sambre, Macedonia 1915–17.

Norway 1940, Fontenay le Pesnil, North West Europe 1944–5, Argoub Sellah, Sicily 1943, Salerno, Minturno, Anzio, Gemmano Ridge, Burma 1942.

LATER LINEAGE

A four-battalion regiment, The Light Infantry was reduced to three battalions in 1969 and to two battalions in 1993.

MUSEUMS

The King's Own Yorkshire Light Infantry Museum, Doncaster Museum and Art Gallery, Chequer Road, Doncaster DN1 2AE (telephone: 01302 734293; e-mail: museum@doncaster.gov.uk; website: www.army.mod.uk/ceremonialandheritage/museums).

The 1914–18 memorial to the 5th Battalion of The King's Own Yorkshire Light Infantry in the Regimental Museum at Doncaster.

The West Yorkshire Regiment (The Prince of Wales's Own) (14th Foot)

ORIGINS AND DEVELOPMENT

The 14th Foot was raised in 1685 as Hales's Regiment. It was affiliated to Bedfordshire in 1782 but its colonel, Sir Harry Calvert, who was also the army's Adjutant General, wished to have it affiliated to his own county of Buckinghamshire. Accordingly, the county affiliation was switched with that of the 16th Foot in 1809. It became The Prince of Wales's Own in 1876 and, in 1881, The West Yorkshire Regiment (The Prince of Wales's Own). A 2nd Battalion existed from 1858 to 1948. Amalgamated 1958.

HISTORY

The 14th saw its first active service in Flanders in 1693, serving under King William III and subsequently taking part in the siege and capture of Namur. It served in Ireland throughout the War of Spanish Succession, being recalled to Scotland during the first Jacobite rebellion in 1715. It served at Gibraltar from 1727 to 1742 and, later, like many other regiments, had a spell of marine service. At Famars in Flanders on 23rd May 1794 the 14th helped check the French advance,

141

The shako of an officer of the 14th Foot, worn at Waterloo, 1815.

its colonel ordering his drummers to take up the French revolutionaries' tune, 'Ça Ira', which the French were playing, calling out, 'Come on lads, we'll break them to their own d— tune!'. A 3/14th was raised in Buckinghamshire in 1813 and, due to be disbanded, its mostly young and raw recruits were rushed across the Channel in June 1815, winning the battle honour 'Waterloo' for the regiment. The 1st/14th spent some twenty-three years in India, gaining a Royal Tiger badge in 1831, while the revived 2/14th served in New Zealand. When the Prince of Wales presented new Colours to the 1st Battalion in India in 1876, he gave the regiment the new title of The Prince of Wales's Own. On its way home from India in 1895, the 2nd Battalion was diverted to West Africa for the Third Ashanti War, later also serving in the South African War. Six Victoria Crosses were won by the regiment in the First World War, while the 8th (Leeds Rifles) Battalion was awarded the French Croix de Guerre for its action at Bligny in 1918. Stationed at Quetta in 1935, the 1st Battalion did considerable work rescuing those caught in an earthquake. Both the 1st and 2nd Battalions served in Burma in the Second World War, meeting at Imphal in 1944 when the 2nd Battalion was part of the relief force flown into the 'Imphal Box' and the 1st Battalion part of the original defending force. After service in Malaya during the Emergency, the 1st Battalion took part in the Suez operation in 1956.

VICTORIA CROSSES

South African War (2); First World War (4); Second World War (1). Of these, one is in the Regimental Museum.

NICKNAMES

Calvert's Entire: from Sir Harry Calvert.

BADGE

The White Horse of Hanover was first adopted by the regiment's grenadiers as a mark of favour from King George III when it was quartered in Windsor in 1759. Subsequently, the whole regiment adopted it in 1873.

MOTTO

Nec aspera terrent ('Difficulties do not deter').

FACINGS

White.

REGIMENTAL MARCHES

'Ça Ira'.

The 8th Battalion of The West Yorkshire Regiment after the capture of Montague de Bligny on 28th July 1918.

COLOURS

York Minster; Claydon House, Middle Claydon, Buckinghamshire (3/14th); Bradford Cathedral; Parish Church of Leeds.

MEMORIALS

York Minster; Clouston, Colenso, KwaZulu-Natal, and Lake Chrissie, South Africa (both 2nd Battalion).

BATTLE HONOURS

Namur 1695, Tournay, Corunna, Java, Waterloo, Bhurtpore, Sevastopol, New Zealand, Afghanistan 1879–80, Relief of Ladysmith, South Africa 1899–1902.

Armentières 1914, Neuve Chapelle, Somme 1916 '18, Ypres 1917 '18, Cambrai 1917 '18, Villers Bretonneux, Lys, Tardenois, Piave, Suvla.

Keren, Defence of Alamein Line, Pegu 1942, Yenangyaung 1942, Maungdaw, Defence of Sinzweya, Imphal, Bishenpur, Meiktila, Sittang 1945.

LATER LINEAGE

Amalgamated in 1958 with The East Yorkshire Regiment (The Duke of York's Own) as The Prince of Wales's Own Regiment of Yorkshire.

MUSEUMS

The Prince of Wales's Own Regiment of Yorkshire Regimental Museum, 3 Tower Street, York YO1 9SB (telephone: 01904 662790; fax: 01904 658824).

The York and Lancaster Regiment
(65th and 84th Foot)

The 65th Foot was raised in 1756 from the 2/12th Foot and was affiliated to the North Riding in 1782. The 84th was raised in 1793 and assumed the subsidiary title of The York and Lancaster in 1820. The two were linked as The York and Lancaster Regiment in 1881. Reduced to a single battalion in 1948 but the 2nd Battalion was briefly revived between 1952 and 1955. Disbanded 1968.

HISTORY

The title of the regiment derives not from the cities of York and Lancaster but from the Duchies of York and Lancaster. Indeed, a large part of the Duchy of Lancaster lay within Yorkshire and this was a Yorkshire regiment recruited largely in the area around Sheffield, Rotherham and Barnsley known as Hallamshire. The 65th went overseas to the West Indies in 1758 as part of an expedition to seize Guadaloupe from the French, the island falling to the British in May 1759, followed by a hard campaign against Havana. After service in the American War of Independence the 65th went to Canada in 1784 but was back in the West Indies, helping to seize Martinique, before being forced to surrender on Guadaloupe in October 1794. Two early incarnations of the 84th were disbanded. One raised in 1759 served in India before being disbanded in 1763, and a two-battalion regiment

The oil painting 'The Battle of Tamai, 1884' by G. Douglas Giles is owned by The York and Lancaster Regiment.

was raised from Scottish emigrants to Canada in 1775 but was disbanded in 1784. The third regiment to bear the number went to Ireland in 1794 but was then sent to Holland that same year before going on to India in 1799. A 2nd Battalion of the 84th was formed in 1808 and took part in the Walcheren expedition and the Peninsular actions of the Nive and Nivelle. It was disbanded in 1819 after guarding convict transports. The 65th also served at the Cape and in India, earning the unique battle honour of 'Arabia' when despatched to reduce piracy in the Persian Gulf in 1809. A detachment of the 84th, which had arrived in the subcontinent in 1842, formed part of the garrison of Cawnpore when the Indian Mutiny broke out in May 1857. Besieged in an entrenchment for three weeks with little water, the garrison surrendered on a promise of safe conduct from the Nana Sahib, only to be massacred as they moved to boats on the Ganges on 27th June 1857. The two hundred or so surviving women and children incarcerated in a house known as the Bibigurh were then slaughtered at the approach of a British relief column on 16th July. After completing seventeen years in India in 1859, the 84th was saluted by the gun battery at Fort William as it sailed home from Calcutta. In 1884 the 1st Battalion served at Suakin, fighting at El Teb on 29th February and Tamai on 13th March. The regiment owns G. Douglas Giles's magnificent contemporary painting of the 1st Battalion at Tamai. The 2nd Battalion took part in the First Boer War and the 1st Battalion in the Second Boer War, a number of men becoming rough riders. During the First World War, of the twenty-two battalions, eight were involved on the Somme on 1st July 1916. The 12th Battalion (the Sheffield Pals) and the 13th and 14th Battalions (the 1st and 2nd Barnsley Pals) all went over the top at Serre. The Sheffield Pals, who had arrived in France just eighteen days before the attack, had 513 officers and men killed, wounded or missing. Eleven battalions saw action in the Second World War. The 1st Battalion was in Norway, suffering heavily in the retreat to Aandalsnes, and fought later in Sicily and Italy. The 2nd Battalion went through the Greek campaign and the loss of Crete in May 1941, being evacuated from Heraklion. Later, it took part in the siege of Tobruk and the second Chindit operation in Burma.

VICTORIA CROSSES
Third Maori War (2); Indian Mutiny (6); First World War (4); Second World War (1). Of these, nine are in the Regimental Museum.

NICKNAMES
The Cat and Cabbage: from the badge.
The Twin Roses: from the red and white roses of York and Lancaster.
The Tigers: from the badge.
The Young and Lovelies: from the letters 'Y' and 'L' of 'York' and 'Lancaster'.

BADGE
The Ducal Coronet and Union Rose came from the 84th, while the Royal Tiger was awarded to the 65th for its long service in India.

MOTTO
Honi soit qui mal y pense ('Let him who thinks evil of it be ashamed').

CUSTOMS
On 22nd April 1940 the 1st Battalion was carried to Norway on HMS *Sheffield* and the same ship brought back the survivors from the disastrous campaign on 30th April. A close association was maintained thereafter between ship and regiment and,

in 1943, the regiment received the freedom of the City of Sheffield already accorded the ship.

FACINGS
White.

REGIMENTAL MARCHES
'The Jockey of York' (1st Battalion).
'The York and Lancaster' (2nd Battalion).

COLOURS
Sheffield Cathedral.

MEMORIALS
Sheffield Cathedral; Ranmoor Church, Sheffield; the Parish Churches of Barnsley and Rotherham; St Mary's Church, Dover; Sheffield Memorial Park, Luke Copse, Serre, Somme, France (12th, 13th and 14th Battalions); Rangeworthy, Spion Kop (Spioenkop), KwaZulu-Natal, South Africa (1st Battalion).

BATTLE HONOURS
Guadaloupe 1759, Martinique 1794, India 1796–1819, Nive, Peninsula, Arabia, New Zealand, Lucknow, Tel-el-Kebir, Egypt 1882 '84, Relief of Ladysmith, South Africa 1899–1902.

Ypres 1915 '17 '18, Somme 1916 '18, Messines 1917 '18, Passchendaele, Cambrai 1917 '18, Lys, Selle, Piave, Macedonia 1915–18, Gallipoli 1915.

Fontenay le Pesnil, Antwerp-Turnhout Canal, Tobruk 1941, Mine de Sedjenane, Sicily 1943, Salerno, Minturno, Crete, North Arakan, Chindits 1944.

MUSEUMS
The York and Lancaster Regiment Museum, The Central Library and Arts Centre, Walker Place, Rotherham, South Yorkshire S65 1JH (telephone: 01709 823635; fax: 01709 823631; website: www.rma.org.uk).

APPENDIX 1: THE AMALGAMATED REGIMENTS

The Devonshire and Dorset Regiment, 1958–
Service has included Northern Ireland and Bosnia.
Museum: *The Military Museum of Devon and Dorset*, The Keep Military Museum, The Keep, Bridport Road, Dorchester, Dorset DT1 1RN (telephone: 01305 264066; fax: 01305 250373; website: www.keepmilitarymuseum.org).

The King's Own Royal Border Regiment, 1959–
Service has included Aden and Cyprus. The regiment was awarded the Wilkinson Sword of Peace for its role in Northern Ireland in 1994 and again for Macedonia in 1998.
Museum: *The Museum of The Border Regiment and The King's Own Royal Border Regiment*, Queen Mary's Tower, Carlisle Castle, Carlisle, Cumbria CA3 8UR (telephone: 01228 532774; website: www.army.mod.uk/ceremonialandheritage /museums).

The King's Regiment, 1969–
(including The King's Regiment [Manchester and Liverpool], 1959–69)
Service has included tours of Northern Ireland and Belize.
Museum: City Soldiers, The King's Regiment Collection, Regional History Section, *Museum of Liverpool*, Pier Head, Liverpool L3 1PZ (telephone: 0151 478 4080; website: www.nmgm.org.uk/liverpoollife).

The Light Infantry, 1968–
(including The Somerset and Cornwall Light Infantry, 1959–68)
Service has included Northern Ireland, Bosnia, Kosovo, Sierra Leone and Afghanistan.
Museum: *The Light Infantry Museum*, Peninsula Barracks, Romsey Road, Winchester, Hampshire SO23 8TS (telephone: 01962 828550; fax: 01962 828534; website: www.army.mod.uk/ceremonialandheritage/museums).

The Prince of Wales's Own Regiment of Yorkshire, 1958–
Service included Aden in 1967.
Museum: *The Prince of Wales's Own Regiment of Yorkshire Regimental Museum*, 3 Tower Street, York YO1 1SB (telephone: 01904 662790; fax: 01904 658824; website: www.army.mod.uk/ceremonialandheritage/museums).

The Princess of Wales's Royal Regiment (Queen's and Royal Hampshire), 1992–
(including The Queen's Regiment, 1966–92 and The Queen's Own Buffs, The Royal Kent Regiment, 1961–6)
Service has included Northern Ireland, Bosnia and Kosovo.
Museum: *The Princess of Wales's Royal Regiment and Queen's Regiment Museum*, Dover Castle, Dover, Kent CT16 1HU (telephone: 01227 818053; website: www.army.mod.uk/ceremonialandheritage/museums).

The Queen's Lancashire Regiment, 1970–
(including The Lancashire Regiment, 1958–70)
The regiment was the last British unit to serve in Berlin, in 1992–4.
Museum: *Museum of The Queen's Lancashire Regiment*, Fulwood Baracks, Preston,

Lancashire PR2 8AA (telephone: 01772 260362; fax: 01772 260583).

The Royal Anglian Regiment, 1964–
(including The 1st East Anglian Regiment, 1959–64, The 2nd East Anglian Regiment [Duchess of Gloucester's Own Royal Lincolnshire and Northamptonshire], 1960–4, and The 3rd East Anglian Regiment, 1958–64)
Service has included Sierra Leone and Afghanistan.
Museum: *The Royal Anglian Regiment Museum*, Land Warfare Hall, Imperial War Museum Duxford, Cambridge CB2 4QR (telephone: 01223 835000, extension 298; fax: 01223 835120).

The Royal Gloucestershire, Berkshire and Wiltshire Regiment, 1994–
(including The Duke of Edinburgh's Royal Regiment, 1959–94)
Service of the Duke of Edinburgh's Royal Regiment included relief operations in the Bahamas in 1960, aid to the civil power in British Guiana in 1961, and peace-keeping operations in Cyprus in 1964. The regiment has since served in Bosnia and Kosovo.
Museum: *The Royal Gloucestershire, Berkshire and Wiltshire Regiment (Salisbury) Museum*, The Wardrobe, 58 The Close, Salisbury, Wiltshire SP1 2EX (telephone: 01722 414536; fax: 01722 421626; e-mail: curator@thewardrobe.org.uk; website: www.thewardrobe.org.uk).

The Royal Greenjackets, 1966–
The regiment has served in the Gulf, Bosnia and Kosovo.
Museum: *The Royal Greenjackets Museum*, Peninsula Barracks, Romsey Road, Winchester, Hampshire SO23 8TS (telephone: 01962 828459).

The Royal Regiment of Fusiliers, 1968–
The regiment undertook thirty-three tours in Northern Ireland between 1969 and 2002 and has also seen service in the Gulf War and in Bosnia.
No separate museum.

The Staffordshire Regiment (The Prince of Wales's), 1959–
The regiment served with the 7th Armoured Brigade in the Gulf War and has since been in Kosovo.
Museum: *The Staffordshire Regiment Museum*, Whittington Barracks, Lichfield, Staffordshire WS14 9PY (telephone: 0121 311 3229; website: www.army.mod.uk /ceremonialandheritage/museums).

The Worcestershire and Sherwood Foresters Regiment (29/45 Foot), 1970–
Service has included Northern Ireland and Bosnia.
No separate museum.

APPENDIX 2: MAJOR WARS AND EXPEDITIONS INVOLVING THE BRITISH ARMY

First Anglo-Dutch War (1652–4)
Second Anglo-Dutch War (1665–7)
Third Anglo-Dutch War (1672–4)
Nine Years War (or War of the League of Augsburg) (1689–97)
War of Spanish Succession (1702–14)
War of Jenkins's Ear (1739)
War of Austrian Succession (1742–8)
Seven Years War (1756–63)
First Mysore War (1767–9)
American War of Independence (1775–83)
First Maratha War (1778–82)
Second Mysore War (1780–4)
Third Mysore War (1790–2)
French Revolutionary and Napoleonic Wars (1793–1815)
Third Kaffir (Cape Frontier) War (1799–1803)
First Kandyan War (1803–4)
Second Maratha War (1803–5)
Fourth Kaffir (Cape Frontier) War (1811–12)
Anglo-American War (1812–14)
Second Kandyan War (1814–15)
Nepalese War (1814–16)
Third Maratha or Pindari War (1816–19)
Third Kandyan War (1817–18)
Fifth Kaffir (Cape Frontier) War (1818–19)
First Burma War (1824–6)
Sixth Kaffir (Cape Frontier) War (1834–5)
First Afghan War (1839–42)
First China War (1839–42)
Conquest of Scinde (1843)
Gwalior Campaign (1843)
First Sikh War (1845–6)
Second China War (1846–7)
First Maori War (1846–7)
Seventh Kaffir (Cape Frontier) War (1846–7)
Second Sikh War (1848–9)
Eighth Kaffir (Cape Frontier) War (1850–3)
Second Burma War (1852–3)
Crimean War (1854–6)
Persian War (1856–7)
Third China War (1856–60)
Indian Mutiny (1857–8)
Second Maori War (1860–1)
Third Maori War (1863–6)
Bhutan War (1864–6)
Abyssinian Expedition (1867–8)
Looshai Expedition (1871–2)
Second Ashanti War (1873–4)
Ninth Kaffir (Cape Frontier) War (1877–8)

Jowakhi Campaign (1877–8)
Second Afghan War (1878–80)
Zulu War (1879)
First Boer War (1880–1)
Conquest of Egypt (1882)
Suakin Expedition (1884–5)
Gordon Relief Expedition (1884–5)
Third Burma War (1885–6)
Sikkim Expedition (1888)
Black Mountain Expedition (1888)
Manipur Expedition (1891)
Relief of Chitral (1895)
Third Ashanti War (1895–1900)
Matabeleland and Mashonaland Rebellion (1896)
Reconquest of the Sudan (1896–8)
Benin Expedition (1897)
North West Frontier Rising (1897–8)
South African War (1899–1902)
Boxer Rebellion (1900)
First World War (1914–18)
Third Afghan War (1919)
Anglo-Irish War (1919–21)
Iraqi Revolt (1920–1)
Arab Revolt (1936–9)
Second World War (1939–45)
Malayan Emergency (1948–60)
Korean War (1950–3)
Kenyan Emergency (1952–60)
Cyprus Emergency (1955–9)
Suez Affair (1956)
Brunei Revolt (1962)
Indonesian/Malaysian Confrontation (1962–6)
Aden and the Radfan (1964–7)
Northern Ireland 'Troubles' (1969–)
Dhofar War (1970–5)
Falklands War (1982)
First Gulf War (1990–1)
Second Gulf War (2003)

APPENDIX 3: BATTLE HONOURS

Tangier (1661–84)
Tangier

Nine Years War (1689–97)
Namur

War of Spanish Succession (1702–14)
Blenheim
Gibraltar
Malplaquet
Oudenarde
Ramillies

War of Austrian Succession (1742–8)
Dettingen

Seven Years War (1756–63)
Guadaloupe
Havannah
Louisburg
Martinique
Minden
Moro
Plassey
Quebec
Wilhemstahl

Mysore Wars (1767-9, 1780–4, 1790–2)
India
Mysore
Seringapatam

Maratha Wars (1778–82, 1803–5, 1816–19)
Ally Ghur
Bhurtpore
Deig
Delhi 1803
Hindoostan
India 1796–1819
Leswarree

American War of Independence (1775–83)
St Lucia

French Revolutionary and Napoleonic Wars (1793–1815)
Albuhera
Almarez
Arabia
Arroyo dos Molinos
Badajoz
Barossa
Busaco
Cape of Good Hope
Copenhagen

Corunna
Ciudad Rodrigo
Dominica
Duoro
Egmont-op-Zee
Fuentes d'Onoro
Guadaloupe
Java
Maida
Marabout
Martinique
Monte Video
Nieuport
Nive
Nivelle
Orthes
Peninsula
Pyrenees
Rolica
St Lucia
St Sebastian
Salamanca
Surinam
Talavera
Tarifa
Toulouse
Tournay
Vimierio
Vittoria
Waterloo

Anglo-American War (1812–14)
Bladensburg
Niagara
Queenstown

Burma Wars (1824–6, 1852–3, 1885–6)
Ava
Burma
Pegu

China Wars (1839–42, 1846–7, 1856–60)
Canton
Pekin
Taku Forts

Afghan Wars (1839–42, 1878–80, 1919)
Afghanistan
Ahmed Khel
Ali Masjid
Cabool
Candahar
Charasia
Ghuznee
Kabul

Kandahar
Khelat
Peiwar Kotal

Gwalior and Scinde (1843)
Hyderabad
Maharajpore
Meeanee
Punniar
Scinde

Sikh Wars (1845–6, 1848–9)
Aliwal
Chillianwallah
Ferozeshah
Goojerat
Moodkee
Mooltan
Mooltjan
Punjaub
Sobraon

*Kaffir (Cape Frontier) Wars (1846–7,
1850–3, 1877–8)*
South Africa

Maori Wars (1846–7, 1860–1, 1863–6)
New Zealand

Crimean War (1854–6)
Alma
Inkerman
Sevastopol

Persian War (1856–7)
Bushire
Koosh-ab
Persia
Reshire

Indian Mutiny (1857–8)
Central India
Delhi
Lucknow

Abyssinian Expedition (1867–8)
Abyssinia

Zulu War (1879)
South Africa

Egypt and the Sudan (1882–98)
Abu Klea
Atbara
Egypt
Hafir
Khartoum
Kirbekan

Nile
Suakin
Tel-el-Kebir
Tofrek

North West Frontier (1895–1919)
Baluchistan
Chitral
North West Frontier India
Tirah

South African War (1899–1902)
Defence of Kimberley
Defence of Ladysmith
Modder River
Paardeburg
Relief of Kimberley
Relief of Ladysmith
South Africa

First World War – Western Front
Aisne
Albert
Amiens
Ancre
Ancre Heights
Armentières
Arras
Bapaume
Bazentin
Bligny
Bois de Buttes
Cambrai
Courtrai
Epehy
Festubert
France and Flanders
Frezenberg
Gheluvelt
Givenchy
Havrincourt
Hill 60
Hindenburg Line
Hooge
Kemmel
La Bassée
Langemarck
Le Cateau
Loos
Lys
Marne
Messines
Mons
Namur
Neuve Chapelle
Nonne Bosschen
Passchendaele
Pilckem

Pursuit to Mons
Retreat from Mons
St Julien
St Quentin
St Quentin Canal
Sambre
Scarpe
Selle
Soissonnais-Ourcq
Somme
Tardenois
Valenciennes
Villers Bretonneux
Vimy
Ypres

First World War – Dardanelles
Gallipoli
Landing at Helles
Landing at Suvla
Sari Bair
Suvla

First World War – Palestine, Mesopotamia and Africa
Baghdad
Ctesiphon
Defence of Kut al Amara
Egypt
El Mughar
Gaza
Jerusalem
Khan Baghdadi
Kilimanjaro
Kut al Amara
Megiddo
Mesopotamia
Palestine
Rumani
Shaiba
Shargat
Tell Asur
Tigris

First World War – Italy and Macedonia
Doiran
Italy
Macedonia
Piave
Struma
Vittorio Veneto

Second World War – North West Europe
Aam
Aller
Antwerp
Antwerp-Turnhout Canal
Arnhem

Bourguebus Ridge
Bremen
Brinkum
Brioux Bridgehead
Caen
Cassel
Cleve
Defence of Arras
Defence of Escaut
Dunkirk
Dyle
Falaise
Fontenay le Pesnil
Geilenkirchen
Gheel
Goch
Hechtel
Hill 112
Hochwald
Lower Maas
Maltot
Mont Pincon
Nederrijn
Normandy Landing
North West Europe
Norway
Noyers
Odon
Ourthe
Pegasus Bridge
Rauray
Reichswald
Rhine
Rhineland
Roer
St Omer-la-Bassée
St Valery-en-Caux
Schaddenhof
Scheldt
Seine
Souleuvre
Tilly-sur-Seulles
Tournhout Canal
Venraij
Villers Bocage
Weeze
Wormhoudt
Ypres-Comines Canal
Zetten

Second World War – Africa and Middle East
Abyssinia
Africa
Akarit
Alam el Halfa
Alem Hamza
Argoub Sellah
Belhamed

Capture of Tobruk
Cauldron
Defence of Alamein Line
Defence of Habbaniya
Defence of Tobruk
Djebel bou Aoukaz
Djebel Kesskiss
El Alamein
Enfidaville
Gazala
Gueriat El Aatch Ridge
Hunt's Gap
Keren
Longstop Hill
Madagascar
Mareth
Medenine
Medjez el Bab
Medjez Plain
Merjayum
Mine de Sedjename
North Africa
Omars
Palmyra
Qued Zarga
Robaa Valley
Sidi Barrani
Tebourba Gap
Tobruk
Tobruk Sortie
Tunis

Second World War – Mediterranean
Anzio
Argenta Gap
Athens
Campoleone
Capture of Forli
Cariano
Cassino
Centuripe
Coriano
Cosina Canal Crossing
Crete
Damiano
Fiesole
Gargiliano Crossing
Gemmano Ridge
Gothic Line
Incentro
Italy
Lamone Bridgehead
Landing in Sicily
Leros
Malta
Marradi
Minturno
Monte Camino

Monte Ceco
Monte Gameraldi
Monte Grande
Montone
Montorsoli
Mozza Grogna
Primosole Bridge
Regalbuto
Rimini Line
Rome
Salerno
Sangro
Sicily
Trasimene Line
Trigno
Tuori
Villa Grande

Second World War – Far East
Aradura
Batu-Pahat
Bishenpur
Burma
Chindits
Defence of Kohima
Defence of Sinzweya
Fort Dufferin
Hong Kong
Imphal
Jahore
Kohima
Malaya
Mandalay
Maungdaw
Meiktila
Myinmu Bridgehead
Myitson
Ngakyedauk Pass
North Arakan
Nyaungu Bridgehead
Paungde
Pegu
Pinwe
Shweli
Singapore Island
Sittang
Taukyan
Yenangyaung
Yu

Korean War (1950–3)
Imjin
Korea
Kowang-San
Naktong Bridgehead
The Hook

APPENDIX 4: REGIMENTS OF FOOT AND THEIR POST-1881 DESIGNATIONS

1st Foot	The Royal Scots
2nd Foot	The Queen's Royal Regiment (West Surrey)
3rd Foot	The Buffs (The Royal East Kent Regiment)
4th Foot	The King's Own Royal Regiment (Lancaster)
5th Foot	The Royal Northumberland Fusiliers
6th Foot	The Royal Warwickshire Regiment
7th Foot	The Royal Fusiliers (City of London Regiment)
8th Foot	The King's Regiment (Liverpool)
9th Foot	The Royal Norfolk Regiment
10th Foot	The Royal Lincolnshire Regiment
11th Foot	The Devonshire Regiment
12th Foot	The Suffolk Regiment
13th Foot	The Somerset Light Infantry (Prince Albert's)
14th Foot	The West Yorkshire Regiment (The Prince of Wales's Own)
15th Foot	The East Yorkshire Regiment (The Duke of York's Own)
16th Foot	The Bedfordshire and Hertfordshire Regiment
17th Foot	The Royal Leicestershire Regiment
18th Foot	The Royal Irish Regiment
19th Foot	The Green Howards (Alexandra, Princess of Wales's Own Yorkshire Regiment)
20th Foot	The Lancashire Fusiliers
21st Foot	The Royal Scots Fusiliers
22nd Foot	The 22nd (Cheshire) Regiment
23rd Foot	The Royal Welch Fusiliers
24th Foot	The South Wales Borderers
25th Foot	The King's Own Scottish Borderers
26th Foot	1st Battalion, The Cameronians (The Scottish Rifles)
27th Foot	1st Battalion, The Royal Inniskilling Fusiliers
28th Foot	1st Battalion, The Gloucestershire Regiment
29th Foot	1st Battalion, The Worcestershire Regiment
30th Foot	1st Battalion, The East Lancashire Regiment
31st Foot	1st Battalion, The East Surrey Regiment
32nd Foot	1st Battalion, The Duke of Cornwall's Light Infantry
33rd Foot	1st Battalion, The Duke of Wellington's Regiment (West Riding)
34th Foot	1st Battalion, The Border Regiment
35th Foot	1st Battalion, The Royal Sussex Regiment
36th Foot	2nd Battalion, The Worcestershire Regiment
37th Foot	1st Battalion, The Royal Hampshire Regiment
38th Foot	1st Battalion, The South Staffordshire Regiment
39th Foot	1st Battalion, The Dorset Regiment
40th Foot	1st Battalion, The South Lancashire Regiment (The Prince of Wales's Volunteers)
41st Foot	1st Battalion, The Welch Regiment
42nd Foot	1st Battalion, The Black Watch (Royal Highland Regiment)
43rd Foot	1st Battalion, The Oxfordshire and Buckinghamshire Light Infantry
44th Foot	1st Battalion, The Essex Regiment
45th Foot	1st Battalion, The Sherwood Foresters (Nottinghamshire and Derbyshire Regiment)

46th Foot	2nd Battalion, The Duke of Cornwall's Light Infantry
47th Foot	1st Battalion, The Loyal Regiment (North Lancashire)
48th Foot	1st Battalion, The Northamptonshire Regiment
49th Foot	1st Battalion, The Royal Berkshire Regiment (Princess Charlotte of Wales's)
50th Foot	1st Battalion, The Queen's Own Royal West Kent Regiment
51st Foot	1st Battalion, The King's Own Yorkshire Light Infantry
52nd Foot	2nd Battalion, The Oxfordshire and Buckinghamshire Light Infantry
53rd Foot	1st Battalion, The King's Shropshire Light Infantry
54th Foot	2nd Battalion, The Dorset Regiment
55th Foot	2nd Battalion, The Border Regiment
56th Foot	2nd Battalion, The Essex Regiment
57th Foot	1st Battalion, The Middlesex Regiment (Duke of Cambridge's Own)
58th Foot	2nd Battalion, The Northamptonshire Regiment
59th Foot	2nd Battalion, The East Lancashire Regiment
60th Foot	The King's Royal Rifle Corps
61st Foot	2nd Battalion, The Gloucestershire Regiment
62nd Foot	1st Battalion, The Wiltshire Regiment (Duke of Edinburgh's)
63rd Foot	1st Battalion, The Manchester Regiment
64th Foot	1st Battalion, The North Staffordshire Regiment (The Prince of Wales's)
65th Foot	1st Battalion, The York and Lancaster Regiment
66th Foot	2nd Battalion, The Royal Berkshire Regiment (Princess Charlotte of Wales's)
67th Foot	2nd Battalion, The Royal Hampshire Regiment
68th Foot	1st Battalion, The Durham Light Infantry
69th Foot	2nd Battalion, The Welch Regiment
70th Foot	2nd Battalion, The East Surrey Regiment
71st Foot	1st Battalion, The Highland Light Infantry (City of Glasgow Regiment)
72nd Foot	1st Battalion, The Seaforth Highlanders (Ross-shire Buffs, The Duke of Albany's)
73rd Foot	2nd Battalion, The Black Watch (Royal Highland Regiment)
74th Foot	2nd Battalion, The Highland Light Infantry (City of Glasgow Regiment)
75th Foot	1st Battalion, The Gordon Highlanders
76th Foot	2nd Battalion, The Duke of Wellington's Regiment (West Riding)
77th Foot	2nd Battalion, The Middlesex Regiment (Duke of Cambridge's Own)
78th Foot	2nd Battalion, The Seaforth Highlanders (Ross-shire Buffs, The Duke of Albany's)
79th Foot	The Queen's Own Cameron Highlanders
80th Foot	2nd Battalion, The South Staffordshire Regiment
81st Foot	2nd Battalion, The Loyal Regiment (North Lancashire)
82nd Foot	2nd Battalion, The South Lancashire Regiment (The Prince of Wales's Volunteers)
83rd Foot	1st Battalion, The Royal Ulster Rifles
84th Foot	2nd Battalion, The York and Lancaster Regiment
85th Foot	2nd Battalion, The King's Shropshire Light Infantry
86th Foot	2nd Battalion, The Royal Ulster Rifles
87th Foot	1st Battalion, The Royal Irish Fusiliers
88th Foot	1st Battalion, The Connaught Rangers
89th Foot	2nd Battalion, The Royal Irish Fusiliers

90th Foot — 2nd Battalion, The Cameronians (The Scottish Rifles)

91st Foot — 1st Battalion, The Argyll and Sutherland Highlanders (Princess Louise's)

92nd Foot — 2nd Battalion, The Gordon Highlanders

93rd Foot — 2nd Battalion, The Argyll and Sutherland Highlanders (Princess Louise's)

94th Foot — 2nd Battalion, The Connaught Rangers

95th Foot — 2nd Battalion, The Sherwood Foresters (Nottinghamshire and Derbyshire Regiment)

96th Foot — 2nd Battalion, The Manchester Regiment

97th Foot — 2nd Battalion, The Queen's Own Royal West Kent Regiment

98th Foot — 2nd Battalion, The North Staffordshire Regiment (The Prince of Wales's)

99th Foot — 2nd Battalion, The Wiltshire Regiment (Duke of Edinburgh's)

100th Foot — 1st Battalion, The Prince of Wales's Leinster Regiment (Royal Canadians)

101st Foot — 1st Battalion, The Royal Munster Fusiliers

102nd Foot — 1st Battalion, The Royal Dublin Fusiliers

103rd Foot — 2nd Battalion, The Royal Dublin Fusiliers

104th Foot — 2nd Battalion, The Royal Munster Fusiliers

105th Foot — 2nd Battalion, The King's Own Yorkshire Light Infantry

106th Foot — 2nd Battalion, The Durham Light Infantry

107th Foot — 2nd Battalion, The Royal Sussex Regiment

108th Foot — 2nd Battalion, The Royal Inniskilling Fusiliers

109th Foot — 2nd Battalion, The Prince of Wales's Leinster Regiment (Royal Canadians)

INDEX